SHAKING OFF THE DUST:
Personal Narratives of Triumph

SHAKING OFF THE DUST

ISBN 978-0-578-77483-1

Cover Design - Sharon Phillip
Graphic and Motion Designer
Cr8-tive Company, LLC

Photography by MLA graphics
www.mlagraphics.com

Printed in United States of America, Atlanta, GA

Published by Sistah Scribes LP
www.sistahscribes.com

Whoever does not receive you, nor hear your words, as you go out of that house or city, shake the dust off your feet.

Matthew 10: 14

New American Standard Bible

Shaking Off The Dust:
Personal Narratives of Triumph
is dedicated to

Peggy J. Alston
7/14/1951 - 12/19/2015

In memory of her zest and love for writing, and her bold and adventurous style which left others touched and inspired.

To the courageous women the world over, who dared to ignite the flame of fearless creativity, and allowed their truths to be heard.

To the African American Women, Men, and children unjustly killed by police officers.
1619-2020

ACKNOWLEDGMENTS

We give thanks to Divine Inspiration, out of which came this volume of stories. We are indebted to our ancestors for their sacrifices, courage, and gifts that guide us with the stories they chose to tell. Our stories are a continuation of their struggles and triumphs. We appreciate our families for their support of yet another opportunity we have agreed to embark on.

We know that nothing like this effort is done by one person working alone. Our work involved help and assistance from others, for which we are tremendously grateful.

We offer heartfelt thanks to our editors Kalin Thomas, Sabbaye McGriff, Marcia Cross-Briscoe, and Wayne South Smith.

Thanks to photographer, Monique Armstrong, for pictures that show us in the best light.

Thank you, Sharon Phillip, Founder/Freelance Designer,

Cr8-tive Company LLC, for creating our beautiful website. www.cr8-tive.co

We honor noted theologians, Rev. Dr. Carolyn McCrary, and Rev. Dr. Gerald Durley, who have worked tirelessly to heal lives, communities, and the earth through teaching, preaching, and activism. We share their commitment to leave this world better than they found it. So, we thank you, Rev. Dr. Durley and Rev. Dr. McCrary for taking time out of your busy schedule to give your support, insight, and endorsement of our book.

Angella Vincentie Bramwell to Akinya Moore-Johnson -- Thank you, my daughter, and my mirror for being a bright light in my life.

Sheryl Johnson -- Thank you, Mom, for giving me life. Sabbaye, I appreciate you for your editing and for your support and guidance.

Patricia Desamours -- Thanks, family, for your love and support. I thank you, Kalin, for your skillful editing and encouragement.

DeAnna Park Jones -- Thank you to my beautiful children, Demetria, Robert, and William, for all the ways you support me and show me your love.

Marcia White Laster -- I salute Stephen White, whose legacy of brilliance, courage, and truth-telling still lives on. I acknowledge my 'master teachers' who have challenged me and taught me well. I am grateful.

Angela H. Rice -- I thank the memory of you, my beloved Carlos. You continue to inspire me. I am grateful to my mother, Edith Turner Harrington, for her tenacity and connection to a powerful tribe of men and women who made "a way." Thank you, Marcia, for your encouragement and editing.

Barbara Gray Armstrong -- Joel, I love you and appreciate you. I cannot imagine being on this journey without your love and support since 1965.

INTRODUCTION

Shaking Off the Dust: Personal Narratives of Triumph is a collection of stories that came from these writers' lived experiences. They, collectively known as Sistah Scribes, decided to share parts of their journeys with each other and with the world. Sharing what makes us vulnerable and open to judgment and criticism has not been easy, but it is necessary for our healing.

If we had known what was on our chosen paths early in our lives, would we have taken a different one? It is often said that if we change one thing in our lives, we change the course of our lives. In effect, we alter our whole life. Would we change anything if it changed everything? By that one thing, I mean some tragic or painful incident. Would we if we could?

Our desire is that you will be encouraged through reading our stories of survival and triumphing over situations and concerns that held us captive for many years. We hope you will find inspiration, as you learn how coping with childhood trauma, decided one woman's career. And understand how sexual assault and mental illness affect family dynamics. Realize the effects of police insensitivity and lack of training to work with the mentally ill on a family as you read what one writer did to cope with the pain of losing her brother at the hands of law enforcement. Many women face problems with infertility as they attempt to have a child. One woman tells her story of how she met her situation head-on and made peace with it when she realized that she would be denied the family she dreamed of.

Think of "dust" as a metaphor for all the unwanted issues that confront us as we strive to live our lives. Whether these matters concern health, family, or work, they are like the accumulation of dust that, with time and effort, can be shaken off. When we were children running and playing all day, literal dust was of no concern to us. A little dust on our clothing did not stop us; we could simply shake it off and continue enjoying our playtime.

But as our youth slipped away, responsibilities, worries, problems, and sometimes seemingly insurmountable circumstances became the dust of adult life. Shaking it off became much harder. Not only does dust get on clothing, but it also gets into the eyes and obscures sight and clouds vision, thereby preventing us from seeing clearly. Worries and concerns can blind us to what we must face; therefore, until we rid ourselves of the dust we have collected, we cannot see solutions that can aid us in making the progress that we desire.

We believe that each person is on her or his own journey, and that healing is an individual matter. How one copes with a situation is as unique as the individual. Life can place heavy burdens on us in childhood and our teen years before we have developed coping skills. Therefore, we encourage anyone who is feeling stressed by their dust to search out the help they need to overcome their circumstance. Today, there are many community resources to turn to if your dust becomes too much for you to handle alone.

Shaking Off the Dust: Personal Narratives of Triumph
is for everyone who has experienced trials or knows
someone who has. The situations considered in this book
are familiar to many yet can be complicated to overcome.
They are the personal accounts of seven women who
narrate incidents of survival, coping, healing, and triumph
with candor.

"Not everything that is faced can be changed, but nothing can be changed until it is faced."

~ James Baldwin

CONTENTS

1

Our Brother's Keeper

Families are meant to be loving and strong, united in each other's good. This is what I was taught, and I know that my family, like many others, is supportive of each other. Sometimes this is easy, and sometimes it can be trying and even painful, and sometimes we question our responsibility to each other. But in the end, our family, my parents and my three siblings were and are our brother's keeper.

My older brother, Stephen, was kind and caring, loving and gentle, brilliant, a Regent's and National Merit Award scholar, funny and articulate. He was a poet, a deep thinker, and a civil rights activist, joining the youth group of the Congress of Racial Equality (C.O.R.E.) at 15 years old. Growing up, he was my mentor, friend, protector, and hero. He also had schizophrenia.

When I was 12 years old, he was 17, he became ill, and I became confused. Who was this person? His illness made him distant, angry, and frustrated about what was happening to him, and oblivious to its effect on those around him. When he had hallucinations and delusions, he believed people in and outside of our family were talking negatively about him and that we, his family, were against him and believed him to be a failure. At times during his illness, there were flashes of the old, loving, brilliant, compassionate brother who was helpful and uplifting.

As challenging as coping with my beloved brother's illness was for our family, his senseless death at age 35 from a police officer's gunshot was more devastating than his illness ever was.

From the time of his diagnosis and for many years, Stephen struggled to accept that he was ill and that his family was not making it all up. He had a period when he was very sick and had to be hospitalized. It took time for him to believe that a psychiatrist could help him and even longer to find the right psychiatrist for him. This wasn't

2

easy as he was on public assistance by then, and most good psychologists and psychiatrists did not work for free or for what Medicaid would pay them. He did eventually get the on-going psychological help he needed after finding a black male therapist whom he trusted and listened to. As a result, he slowly began to improve. He came to realize his beliefs caused by his illness were not real. This therapist cared about him and did not pity him or think of him as a scary black man. He struggled, but they built trust in each other over many years. During that time, he was taking several medications and supplements to help him function and to eliminate the hallucinations.

Stephen desperately wanted a healthy life, to finish college, and to work. He had periods when he was ill, but in his last seven years, Stephen experienced more extended periods when he was better, seeing his therapist, taking his medicines, and doing well. He was able to finish undergraduate school, get a scholarship and attend Stonybrook University with a graduate assistantship in a joint master's and doctoral program in American Studies, and have a social life.

Before that, during my teen years, I learned to wear the "I am fine" mask so as not to worry my parents, who were consumed with his illness and had enough on their plates. My brother's illness took a financial and emotional toll on our family. I tried to be invisible and not rock the boat at home with my emotional needs, desires, and typical teenage angst about dating, clothes, friendships, and school. I would not bring friends to our house because I never knew when Stephen would act out. Although he was never violent, it was uncomfortable and scary at times because you never knew when his hallucinations or delusions would surface. I was responsible, mature, and understanding from an early age, but there were times when I felt resentful and angry. At those times, I felt justified in my feelings, but also guilty. Was I selfish or just needing self-care as I matured into a young woman?

My sister, who is eight years older than me, was very close to Stephen. But she was out of the house and in college when he became ill. She is an accomplished

4

psychotherapist, and I believe Stephen's illness influenced her career decision. I also have a brother who is six years younger than me. He is a high school literature teacher studying for his doctorate in education. Like my older brother was to me, I was my younger brother's mentor, friend, and protector. After all, I was 'his' big sister.

We had and still have a close, loving relationship. When Stephen became ill, I took on more responsibility for my younger brother, supporting him, trying to be there as a buffer between him and our older brother, and helping us both have as normal a life as possible. I never resented caring for him. I knew that love required an unselfish commitment. I felt my parents had so much to handle with Stephen that I needed to take on some of the responsibility of raising my younger brother. When I went off to college, I was happy to escape the situation at home, but I also felt concerned about leaving my younger brother alone at home without me.

When Stephen became ill in 1964, the understanding of his illness was limited, and the medications available were Draconian. Over time, the research and public understanding of the disease and the medicines to treat it have evolved. As a result of the psychological help my parents got him, they were all hopeful he could attend college. Even before affirmative action, as a high school senior in 1965, he was accepted to Columbia University, Bard College, and Williams College, all with academic scholarships. He decided to attend Williams and was one of 18 black men among the 1000 students attending the college. His first year there was a rough one. His illness worsened, and he had to withdraw after his freshman year.

Early in his illness, Stephen was so sedated he could hardly function. When I visited him during the year and a half that he was hospitalized, he was like a zombie. The environment was strange and very institutional, not homey or comforting at all. Afterward, he came home and continued medication and psychiatric support. Later, my mother did a great deal of research, and in conjunction with the doctor, changed his medications to ones that did not have such a debilitating effect on him. She was his biggest cheerleader. My mother insisted he take vitamins and supplements to help support him and eat foods that were as natural as possible. She innately knew this would help him even though the doctors were not convinced. He did benefit from these measures. From this, I gained an interest in vitamins, herbs, and eating clean and close to nature, which I continue even today. This is one of the positives that came from my brother's illness.

At home, Stephen spent lots of time in his room, reading, writing poetry, and sleeping from the medication. Sometimes he was delusional and brooding. My family members are avid readers, including Stephen, who loved all kinds of literature, history, science, and politics. When I was young, he would often read to me, sometimes in dialect, which I adored. He loved to read classic literature, but he also loved folk literature, like the black folktales of

Uncle Remus. These were written in dialect and challenging to read, but not for Stephen. From him, I developed a passion for black history, the literature of black authors, and writing. He became very accomplished as a writer. After his death, my sister submitted some of his poems to magazines. Several were published, including two in *Essence Magazine*.

It took me years during the time I lived at home, and went off to college, and even after my brother's death in 1982, to stop being resentful for what his illness did to our family and him—how it robbed us of any sense of normalcy and him of reaching his potential. I had to learn to forgive him, my parents, and myself.

There were times during his illness when Stephen was very loving and protective. Then there were occasions when the delusions and hallucinations made him hell to be around. Both taught me a lot. After my first year at college, I came home for the summer while Stephen was still living at home. He was withdrawn and pensive. On one occasion, I had a nosebleed, and it would not stop. My father felt I needed to go to the hospital, and I agreed. Stephen had been observing the situation and came over and gently lifted me and carried me to the car, so my parents could take me to the hospital to have my nose packed. He hugged

8

me after he placed me in the car and told me it would be alright. I knew I would be OK, so I was not worried. What I remember clearly, and what made an impression on me, was my brother's care and love for me during his illness.

On another occasion, I came home to visit after my brother had moved out to a rented room. He came by my parent's home to do his laundry. My dad was at work. Stephen was agitated, belligerent, and delusional. He was loud and angry with my mom over an imagined wrong. My mom is a strong woman, but this time his behavior was upsetting her. It was bothering me also, but I was more concerned about and protective of Mom. I recall that I intervened, told him he was wrong about Mom, and asked him to leave. He stormed out of the house. Both of these incidents reinforced my understanding of love—love from and for my family. These and other incidents helped me develop the strength and resilience to stand for the truth and what is right. It also undergirded my foundation of love.

Growing up with my brother's illness left me withdrawn and not feeling very valued or confident. While in college and maturing, I learned to value myself more because I was a responsible person that people could depend on, and I liked that. I was always an excellent student, having been inducted into the National Honor Society in high school. Several students asked me to study with them and help them with their writing. Being a detailed, organized, and caring person, this was easy for me, and I enjoyed supporting them.

I had my share of jobs in college, flipping burgers, and doing bookkeeping at Liberty Mutual Insurance Company. From these jobs, I earned spending money and paid part of my tuition that my scholarship did not cover. I also had a work/study job that placed me at the Children's Museum of Boston. I was hired there to be the back-up floor manager and work with the floor manager to schedule all employees working on the exhibits. I had to learn the museums' programs and ensure that the daily operations, including ticket sales and bank deposits, went well. I loved it. Not only was it related to my education major, but I was learning such interesting information from the museum's collections, and I truly enjoyed working with the staff. When the floor manager left her position, I was asked to take over as the full-time floor manager. I had six months to go before I graduated, though I wanted the job, I was not going to quit school to take it. They really appreciated my work and decided to hold the position for me until I graduated. In the meantime, they hired someone to take the position solely for the interim period until I was available. I was surprised and ecstatic. I was 21 years old and had the certainty of a management job that I loved waiting for me upon graduation. Learning responsibility so early at home had paid off! This was the beginning of a 29- year career in Museum Education and Management.

As I moved on in my career, my brother Stephen was able to move forward as well. He had so much courage. Even though the voices in his head and delusions sometimes overwhelmed him, he came back more determined to achieve his goals. As he improved due to newer medications, family support, diet, and a caring therapist he trusted, he entered Old Westbury College in 1976, an institution dedicated to the education of nontraditional students. He completed undergraduate school. This was a major victory for him, and he was respected and appreciated by his professors for his intelligence, determination, diligence, and passion. He entered Stonybrook University for a joint Masters/Ph.D. program with a full academic scholarship in 1982.

Stephen wrote an essay to obtain the Martin Luther King scholarship from Old Westbury College. He wrote, "I plan to dedicate the remaining years of my life to teach American history as I became aware of it at Old Westbury—that is with emphasis on the forgotten and overlooked role of minorities and women shaping this unique nation. I also plan to write creatively about the black experience in America—something I have been doing since I was sixteen. ... To conclude, I would deem it a great honor to receive the Martin Luther King award and would certainly strive to live the type of life that would be a living testament to this award, Westbury, and Martin Luther King."

In October of 1982, Stephen went into Manhattan to do research for the professor he was working with as part of his graduate assistantship. He stopped to purchase cigarettes at a subway concession stand. The person working at the stand said Stephen did not pay for the cigarettes. Stephen was an incredibly honest man, and we know he paid for them. An argument ensued, and the policeman at the subway station was called. He arrested Stephen and took him into custody.

At the jail, he was not allowed to call us or have the medication he regularly took to eliminate the hallucinations. When he told police officers, it was essential to his health that he takes his medicines, they did not believe him. He was beaten. When he finally got word to us to let us know what had occurred, he had been there a few days. His therapist called the jail to try to get them to give him his medicines. They refused. After another day or so, we got him bail, and he was released. By then, without the medicines and as a result of the abuse, he was paranoid and starting to have delusions and hallucinations.

He came back to our parents' home and resumed taking his medicines. But the damage had been done, and it would take two weeks before the medicines could work again. He was scheduled to return for a court date the next week but believed if he went to court, he would be beaten again and incarcerated. We could not convince him otherwise. He was depressed and delusional, and the night before the court date, he left the house with a knife. My parents called the police to disarm him, as they thought he might hurt himself, not to harm him. Instead, they shot him. They should have used a different approach to subdue him than they use with criminals because my parents had told them he was mentally ill, confused, and had not had medication. But they did not. My younger brother and father were present when the police confronted Stephen. He didn't recognize either of them and called them "dolphins." He was hallucinating.

The police did not try to calm him. They saw a black man with a knife and decided he was a danger. Even though the police could see and hear that he was delusional, they

14

treated him inhumanely. They provoked him. There were a lot of police on the scene. They pinned him against a wall with weapons drawn. Who knows what or who Stephen thought they were? When my brother moved towards them and tried to defend himself, they shot him three times— one bullet to the leg and another in the head. He was put on life support and died three days later.

This is how our so-called civilized society treats the mentally ill.

My family sued Nassau County and the police department, including the five officers involved in his death. We lost the suit. But this is what I find even more disturbing: We contended that the police should have been trained to handle a mentally ill person. The court agreed but denied a real award. They admitted that the police officers should have been better trained and offered an award of $100,000 that they would use to train police. No money would come to us for Stephen's life or his and our family's pain and suffering. They placed no value on a Black man's life. We saw the stipulations of the $100,000 as a slap in the face and did not accept the offer.

After his death, we used contributions from friends and family to establish the Stephen E. White Memorial Book Fund at the College at Old Westbury's library. The Book -Fund was used to enrich the library's collection of African American literature and history. An award was established at Old Westbury in his name and is given every year in the American Studies and Comparative Humanities Department. It is given to students who exhibit "creativity, academic excellence, extraordinary commitment to equality and social justice, and a commitment to fight racism."

Stephen's death devastated our family. He had worked so hard. He had been so courageous. He had overcome his fears and delusions over and over again. In his book, The Seasons of a Man's Life, Daniel Levinson says, "A person's dream is his personal myth, where he is the central character, a would-be hero engaged in a noble quest. The reward is not just fame or fortune, it is living one's life to the fullest and leaving one's mark on the world."

16

Stephen had a disability that kept him from enjoying life as others do, but it did not prevent him from making a valuable impression on all the people who knew him.

For my family, we all struggled in different ways with Stephen's illness and death. I know for me, while I lived at home, I struggled between caregiving and making a life of my own. Being a sibling and not a parent, it was easier for me to disconnect. For my parents, however, caregiving was constant; they could not leave or take a break. When my brother died, they grieved and were forever changed. The parents I had before my brother died were very different than the ones I had after his death. My younger brother and father, who witnessed the shooting, both felt guilty, angry, and powerless. Over time, with help, they healed as best they could. My parents did gain more freedom and began to travel more and make a new chapter for themselves.

I was shocked and angry. It was surreal. I have little respect for the police as a result. Stephen had struggled and worked so hard. He overcame, and now he was gone. It was brutal and unfair.

For many years, I didn't know how to handle these feelings, so I coped by avoidance as much as I could. It was not a beneficial way to cope. You can try to avoid your emotions, but they are still a part of your consciousness and will, at some point, require that you address them. Stuffing them down only makes that emotion stronger. It took me years to realize that it was important to address emotions stirred up by what I call "master teachers." Master teachers are those people in your life that you cannot avoid. They can be your sibling, parent, next-door neighbor, relative, boss, colleague, etc. These are people who challenge you, who you must see regularly, and their words or actions push your buttons and may even make you want to scream. You can try to avoid them at family gatherings, move to a different neighborhood or a different job. But they will follow you until you confront the situation they present maturely and truthfully. They are here for our emotional growth. I do not mean the person literally follows you, but you will notice the same actions, behaviors, or problems with a different person at your new job or in your new neighborhood. "Because wherever you go, there you are."

I never addressed these feelings of anger, confusion, and discomfort thoroughly with my parents, though we did talk. When we suppress or cut off our emotions, we cannot evoke them when we need to use them on our behalf. Later in life, similar incidents kept arising until I stopped avoiding, accepted, and confronted the situation with the next master teacher. At one point, I was so upset by the actions of the master teacher that I dreamed we had a physical fight. The dream was a wake-up call. I stopped being silent. In one situation, the master teacher was a colleague, and in another situation, a boss. I was so shaken by their treatment that I had finally stopped using the avoidance technique and replaced it with speaking my mind, clearly, kindly, and firmly. I took back my power.

I had been running for a while. I ran almost daily, and it raised endorphins and helped my energy to soar, allowing me to cope with my stress and feel more in control of my life, particularly after Stephen's transition. It was a great support in my healing. Running outdoors in nature was a calming spiritual experience. I loved running in Central Park, especially at the more wooded north end, I ran most days before work. I have always been a morning person, and this helped me wake up and turn my energy into a passion for the day's experiences. At work, my staff could always tell when I had been running. I would organize my day while running, and when I arrived at work, I knew exactly how I wanted the day to go and what needed to get done. I ran for exercise and to de-stress, but after my brother's transition, also to heal. I frequently ran many races, including the New York City Marathon, and won trophies for many years no matter where I lived. It was a confidence-building and empowering experience. I loved the feeling. During the '80s to the late '90s, I would have quit my job to run professionally if someone had been willing to pay me. I loved it that much.

In 1977, I was re-introduced to my spirituality and began reading up on New Thought, and eastern religions, including Buddhism and Hinduism. A lot of the concepts intrigued me and made sense to me, more sense than the Episcopalian faith in which I was raised. I scoured the shelves of the East-West bookstore in New York City for books. Thankfully, I had my new spiritual beliefs to hold onto when my brother passed. It helped. But my hurt and anger did not go away. Things seemed so unfair. Life was hard.

In 1986, four years after Stephen's death, I was dating someone who asked me to go to church with him. I hesitated because although I was reading about spirituality, I had not been in a church in years. Traditional religion did not appeal to me. I was searching for a spirituality that I could use every day, that made sense. But my friend insisted this was different. So, I went to church with him. He took me to the Unity Church of Christianity at Avery Fisher Hall, a part of Lincoln Center, where the congregation met on Sundays. Rev. Eric Butterworth was the minister then. When I walked in, I was fascinated by the bookstore set up in the lobby. The tables were filled with hundreds of New Thought titles, including audiotapes of books, lectures, and sermons by New Thought authors and ministers.

Being an avid reader, I loved it. I had found a treasure trove of new information that I was hungry for. Then we entered the service. Avery Fisher hall holds over 2,000 seats, and they were all filled. The service made sense to me. I enjoyed it. It was not like the Episcopal church service that was very ritualistic and always the same. Rev. Butterworth was interesting, and I felt comfortable and at home. It felt right. When the service ended, the congregation sang "Let there be peace on earth and let it begin with me." I began to tear up and had to hold back the tears. It resonated with me. I was home. I had found the church that lived the spiritual practices in the books I had been reading. I did not know such a church existed.

Our life is a series of seasons. How we handle the seasons of our life depends on our attitude. Attitude is everything. My Unity teachings revealed that there is a spiritual solution to every problem. In fact, that is the title of a book by the late Dr. Wayne Dyer, a preeminent New Thought leader. Since I was learning to change my thinking to change my life, I was happier and understood that even the difficult, painful times are blessings. So, I began to see how much living with my brother had made me responsible, more loving, more empathetic, compassionate, and resilient. It also left me with a love of reading, history, language, poetry, and the arts. Stephen's courage and my spirituality have given me courage, dedication, and faith to handle my life journey. I am grateful for his journey and for being his sister. My gratitude for his love, intelligence, compassion, and determination stays with me always. In 2004, after a four-year course of study, I graduated from ministerial school and was ordained as a New Thought minister and spiritual counselor. My ministry touches many of our brothers and sisters. Stephen would be proud. When I think of him now, my heart smiles.

It wasn't always that way. I was angry with him for a long time. It took years for me to be at peace. In the early '90s, a friend told me about the Life Spring program. It was a five-day training that consisted of a series of lectures and participatory processes that were designed to show how we hold ourselves back in life. It was pricey, but I was investing in myself. It was very intense and made me examine my hurts and pains, joys, and triumphs. It was all day and all evening until 11 pm each day. There were breaks, but you were immersed, so you had to focus on what you were trying to change. You had time to meditate (and pray if you like) in a darkened room for a long time. I took the workshop to heal and move forward. So, the sadness, guilt, anger, and pain from my life as Stephen's sister and my parents' handling of it were glaring.

One of the principles of New Thought is that if someone knew better, they would have done better. Until that workshop, this maxim had not helped me dissipate my angry and sad feelings of victim-hood. At the workshop, I finally realized that my parents and my brother all did their best. It was a difficult situation for everyone. There was no handbook to follow. No one was a victim. We were all participants on a shared journey. I worked for hours until I could honestly say I forgave them and, most importantly, myself. It may sound New Age, which a lot of people knock, but it worked for me.

"Our attitude toward our fellow human beings should not be to condemn or judge harshly, but to see the perfect idea resides in them, no matter how grievous the mistake, recognizing that if they knew better, they would do better."-Ernest Holmes

After all, we are all doing the best we can with as much courage and style as we can.

I now think of compassion as care for another, especially if that person is troubled. My brother was troubled but also compassionate and loving. He was a keeper of his brothers (and sisters) also. One of his gifts to me is that, in his honor, I endeavor to be compassionate to all my brothers and sisters on this journey with me. Each of us has something to give. Let each of us give our best from the altar of divine love. Nothing less is acceptable. It will not deplete you. In fact, it will uplift you and bring you joy and fulfillment. Stephen lives on in our hearts, and in the writings, he left us. Here is one of his poems. Enjoy!

Every Thursday at 3:30 pm

you come upon them occasionally
at off-time hours
these old men on bicycles
pedaling to nowhere.

i saw one this morning at 6 am pedaling down the road out of
the fog at a senior denizen's pace
in a basket mounted on the handle
bars were 2 greasy brown paper bags
containing 2 magic apples & a thermos
bottle of ambrosia

when i was ten one of these old men
intrigued me.
every thursday at 3:30 pm he would pedal down the block til he
was directly
across from my house then turn around &
vanish up the road.

i, the poet has a feeling that
they are magical voyagers these old men. & that if one followed
them he would find a pot of gold or vanish abruptly into hades
or soar into heaven.

i would follow one home sometime & have in fact had that urge.

but I'm fearful that if i do i will find out that he is a

grandfather, that his name is
seymour that he worked himself up to head clerk at the A&P
that he is now retired & that
his wife (bless her soul) nags
him constantly about his iron tonic.

(c Stephen White 1979)

2

My Mom, My Life: A Healing Journey

I can remember lifting my mom off the toilet and putting her to bed or getting her up from the kitchen table where she'd passed out, her face just inches away from being submerged in a bowl of soup. One night she came into my room. I glanced over at the clock. It was close to 2 a.m. I asked, "Mom, what are you doing? It's the middle of the night." She replied, "I need to clean." She fiddled around beneath my desk. I reached over and turned on the light. "What are you looking for?" She had the plug in one hand and was holding the vacuum cleaner in the other. "I need to clean," she repeated. I managed to convince her that this wasn't an optimal time and she finally left. This was a typical incident in life lived with a manic depressive.

According to the website 10faq.com, people with manic depression, now known as bipolar disorder, experience mood swings that can occur for no particular reason and swing between manic happiness and suicidal depression. Symptoms include elevated mood, inflated self-esteem, speaking quickly, erratic/suicidal thoughts and behavior, substance abuse, overspending and guilt. Celebrities who have been diagnosed as bipolar include Kanye West, Mariah Carey, Jean Claude Van Damme, Catherine Zeta-Jones, Patty Duke, Vincent Van Gogh and Winston Churchill.

I have memories of my mother's manic episodes from the mid-1960's when I was 15 or so. They lasted up until a few years before her death in 2016 at 95 years old. Sometimes the episodes lasted a few months. Sometimes they went on for more than a year. There were few periods when she was not in a state of manic euphoria, getting little sleep, spending money as if she had a limitless supply and talking endlessly, barely stopping to take a breath. She was very much against taking medication, even refusing to take an aspirin if she had a headache. Her acceptance of medicines came later, when she was in an assisted living home and had someone to administer them. Even then, I can remember visiting her and she would spit them out in front of me as soon as the nurse turned her back. There was always a mental power struggle between me and my mom, and we were always at odds between who knows better and "you can't tell me anything because I know better than you."

I always had a deep and abiding love for my mother but dealing with her illness was an emotional dust that settled into my life in my teenage years and often had me operating in a haze. I learned a lot about becoming a strong woman and became immune to embarrassment. I also acknowledged some of life's pitfalls I didn't want to fall into like losing control of my mind or trusting that marriage would last forever. There were feelings of resentment and I remember thinking about mom's illness in my 30's and wondering "Is it always gonna be like this?" And pretty much it was but I never stopped learning from or loving her.

My mom, Dorothy Stokes Moore was an extraordinary

woman. Beautiful, intelligent, and engaging, she was the epitome of graciousness and when you met her, you were drawn to her instantly. She was raised in a middle-class family in Boston, MA, where she attended good schools, including Girl's Latin School, Radcliffe College, and later on, Howard University. She married my father, William Moore (originally from Birmingham, AL), whose background was also middle class and who was bright enough to have completed Morehouse College in three years, graduating at 19.

Like all good wives, she supported her husband's ambitions, moving to Rochester, NY, where he was employed as a chemical engineer for Kodak (remember camera film?) and where I was born. Soon after, Dad took a job in Manhattan and we moved to the Bronx, initially living with Mom's cousin Althea and her husband Zelton, until my brother was born. Then we moved into our first home in Mount Vernon, NY.

It was Black Camelot. Many weekends were spent having cookouts or with friends or relatives who came over to play bridge or pinochle. We moved into the house when I was about 12, and over the next few years, I lived a pretty idyllic life. Education was always a top priority in my family and at an early age both my brother and I were enrolled in Fieldston, a well-known private school in Riverdale, NY, where we cultivated friendships with wealthy Jews and liberal Protestants. On the weekends, I hung out with my neighborhood buddies, often riding the subway down to Greenwich Village where we would buy dollar earrings and eat pizza at 15 cents per slice.

I remember the day I figured out that something was going on with my mom. I was in my early teens and watching an old movie, "The Three Faces of Eve." I loved the female lead, Joanne Woodward. I thought she was a great actress and she was married to Paul Newman, one of the most handsome actors of all time (and my homeboy from Mount Vernon). The storyline was compelling. Ms. Woodward plays a mousy little woman named Eve White, who was married and had a daughter. When she began behaving strangely, her husband took her to a psychiatrist in a last-

32   SHAKING OFF THE DUST

ditch effort to try and save their marriage.

One day during a therapy session, an alter ego named Eve Black emerged. Now Eve Black was altogether different from Eve White. She was sexy, flirty, gregarious and always out for a good time. I looked at the contrasting personalities in this one woman and I had an epiphany: "My God! That's my mother!" I later learned that Mom's impairment was called bipolar disorder, known back then as manic depression. In the movie, Eve White and Eve Black eventually merged into a third personality, and the story had a happy ending. Unfortunately, that would not be the case for my mom.

The day that everything changed in my world was the day that my father came home from work and announced that he wanted a divorce. He had met a woman on the train while commuting from the City and wanted to be with her. She worked as a fabric designer and was tall, sexy and vivacious. Her voice had a breathy quality and delivery much like Marilyn Monroe and he was in love. Add to this that she had been in love with a man named William

Moore (my father's name) when she was in her 20's but her mother had separated them by sending her off to Paris to study art. It was Kismet.

My mother didn't take it well. Although masters-level educated, she had but one desire in life and that was to be a good wife and a good mother. Initially, she begged him not to break up the family or the marriage of 22 years. She implored him to have the affair and let it run its course, believing he would eventually grow tired of his mistress and somehow regain his senses. But he was having none of it. He reiterated that he had no wish to have an affair but to be with this woman on a full-time basis. The depression that had marked Mom's life since her teens was not aided much by the possibility of raising two kids alone, and with little job experience besides a few years of teaching as a graduate student.

The revelation that Dad was leaving was also compounded by the stark realization that two years before, Mom had undergone surgery for the removal of a benign cyst in her neck, which, when removed also resulted in the severing of

34

a nerve in her face that left her mouth permanently twisted in a semi smirk. So, she was dealing with a permanent facial disability, the prospect of raising two kids and having to reenter the workforce. That's a lot for anyone to deal with. But she did it and got us to school every day and on time until I was old enough to drive. Still, becoming a divorcee was taking its toll. She would make late night calls to friends or family members and cry and cuss about the way she had been treated. It was hard enough dealing with her bouts of mania and depression, but when she began to take regular deliveries from the neighborhood liquor store, that's when things really spiraled out of control.

Over a period of some 20 years, my brother and I had contact with several doctors, all of whom gave the same clinical diagnosis. The issue with my mom was that even though she was thought to be mentally impaired, she wasn't considered a danger to herself or to others. She never got so far out of her head that she was incoherent. Her behavior was erratic and annoying but never far out enough for her to be considered "bat shit crazy." I remember the day my father sat me down after a particularly grueling incident in which she had made her way across town in her bathrobe and slippers to yell obscenities up to his apartment. My father called and my brother and I drove over to get her. In our world, this was just another - day in the life.

"Look" he said, "we've got to do something about her." As if "we" were handling this problem and he was still there. "She's becoming a danger to herself and to others." What he didn't say but clearly meant was that she was also becoming an embarrassment to him and his new wife and he needed it to stop. I remember feeling, "This is my mother you're talking about. What do you expect me to do?" He explained that it was time to have her committed so that she could receive treatment. "I can't be there when they come to get her," I told him, knowing instinctively that I could not witness that scene. I had long since gotten past the point where my mother caused me embarrassment as the emotional dust of her illness settled on my shoulders and seeped into my soul. I understood that she would never be fully capable of managing herself, but my emotions wreaked havoc on me, and I had periods of feeling bitter at why she wasn't "normal" and resentful about her situation being dumped on me without me having a say.

We put her in an institution called Valhalla, close to Poughkeepsie, NY for what was a 10-day observation period. By the end of the 10 days, Mom had gathered personal information on most of the patients as well as half of the staff. She was a master manipulator and an engaging conversationalist, and she knew very well how to draw people in. The doctors brought us in and gave us three options: First, they could release her and advise that she take lithium (the only available medication at the time); They could advise a combination of the meds as well as therapy; or they could admit her to a state facility, which brought to mind visions of scenes from the movie "One Flew Over the Cuckoo's Nest." We took her home with her pledge to take the meds and get therapy and that was it.

She did engage in one therapy session but never took the pills, which we found in her dresser drawer some 30 years later when she sold her home, and everybody went on with their lives.

She could make hurtful comments when in a manic state. In 1973, the first year I was married and living in Washington, DC, I hosted Thanksgiving dinner for Mom, her cousin Althea, whom I called "Aunt," Althea's sister and husband and my in-laws. In the middle of dinner, Mom stood up, announced that she felt she was not being treated well and was ready to go home. My aunties were mortified and tried to calm her and get her to sit down and be quiet, lest my new in laws would discover the level of craziness their son had married into. But I said, "No. If she's not happy, I want her to leave and stop disrupting everyone's dinner." And with that, my Uncle Don, God bless him, got up from the dinner table and took her back to the Greyhound bus station, as bus travel was her preferred transportation mode. It provided her the opportunity to meet someone she called a "nice young man," that she could talk to and who could handle her luggage.

Telemarketers were a godsend for Mom. It was almost the equivalent of shopping on-line. She was always putting money down on a cruise and then trying to figure out who she could convince to embark on the adventure with her. She spent hundreds on clothing and accessories and then inevitably she would crash and fall into a depressive state with no memory of these purchases. She almost lost her house, until her cousin Pearl bailed her out. I think at that point she had a serious talk with herself and decided it was up to her to rein herself in or face the prospect of becoming homeless. This was the mental struggle that was always in play. She convinced herself that she was fully in control. But it was a fairy tale.

From a physical standpoint, Mom appeared to be perfectly normal. Except for her mouth, which, as I mentioned was twisted into a permanent smirk, she came across as charming, opinionated and smart. But once she started talking, it was another matter. To say she had oral diarrhea would be putting it mildly. I told people, "You have to cut her off. She will not stop on her own." But they were often mesmerized and attempting to be polite. And so, many times, I had to end the conversation abruptly, knowing that Mom would continue to talk as long as someone was listening.

Over the years, I began to introduce the concept of manic depression into our conversations. As a Counselor I felt compelled to be honest with her. To help her face what was going on in her mind and what we had all been dealing with for years. As her daughter, I'd grown weary of navigating through Mom's ups and downs and unwillingly riding the mental roller coaster right along with her. I gave her examples and tried to explain things like why her best friend in the neighborhood had walked away from her when she lashed out and called her a lesbian, but Mom was having none of it and intimated that I was lying.

I could not convince her that she was suffering from mental illness because in her mind, there was nothing wrong. This is the dust that works its way into our lives

40

and nudges us to believe that things are okay when we suspect they are not. I've always thought one of the hardest things about dealing with mental illness is the absence of the awareness of it and of the effects it has on one's life. In her mind's eye, I think she felt as if she was dealing with sporadic bouts of depression and nothing more.

By the time she reached her late 70's, Mom began to talk about writing a book. She wanted to tell her own story and she would do it in her own way. She often remarked that she was going to get the story down on sheets of legal pads and then have someone transcribe it for her, but it never happened. I offered to do tape recorded sessions, but she rebuked the idea. I think she worried that somehow, I would take full credit for the book and try to keep all the profits. It was her story and she would have full autonomy over it and that was that.

Family relationships played a big role in keeping Mom on the right track. As with many Black families, I was raised to understand that we must always look out for each other and when crises arise, everyone in the family pitches in to help. Mom's cousin Althea was a godsend in this area. She was always there to lend a helping hand. She and her husband Zelton had no children of their own but they watched out for me and my brother as if they had birthed us. Aunt Althea worked as a domestic for Jewish clients. She was a very giving person and always doing something for somebody else. Uncle Zelton was cool and engaged in activities that I wanted to learn like fishing and golf. He was also my introduction to the Shriner's organization and the mysticism surrounding the Masons.

After Uncle Zelton died, Mom's mental illness progressed, and she began to have paranoid thoughts about Aunt

Althea trying to steal her husband and children. Fortunately for her, Althea ignored Mom's mean comments and ugly rants and never stopped checking on her welfare until she was unable to do so. The other close relatives who were instrumental in keeping tabs on Mom were my father's sister, Margaret, and her husband, Milton. Aunt Margaret taught music in Brooklyn, NY public schools and ruled her household and her husband with a stern guiding hand. "Uncle Miltie," as he was known, was a lawyer who later became a judge and was as laid back as his wife was strict. I always believed that a part of Aunt Margaret's sense of responsibility came from a feeling of guilt at my father having abandoned his marriage after 22 years. She was raised to believe that once you entered into a marital relationship, you were in it for life. And since they had no children of their own, I think that she saw herself as a surrogate in raising her niece and nephew since it was apparent that her sister-in-law would never be capable of doing an adequate job.

Throughout my high school years, my aunt and uncle made at least one trip to our home every month to make sure things were in order and that we weren't about to be set out on the street. I had frequent run ins with my aunt, especially when I felt she was overstepping her boundaries and usurping my mother's territory. I had to gently remind her that I had one set of parents and they were doing a great job. My mother stood behind this as she was often annoyed by how Aunt Tee (as we called her) conducted herself. But my father coddled his older sister and did not like to cross her. She was his sister and he was fiercely protective. Uncle Miltie had a different take on how best to handle the situation. He saw Mom's inner brilliance and it was that side of her to which he catered. They adored each other and when they got together, they would often sit in a corner nursing cocktails and commiserating about how to deal with Margaret's bossy nature.

I remember Aunt Tee phoning me on more than one occasion when I was at college, imploring me to come home because my mother was, once again, out of control. "What am I supposed to do?" I thought. "I'm just trying to make my way through college and that is struggle enough for me right now." But I usually found a way to go because she would lay a guilt trip on me by saying, "That's your mother; this is your responsibility." Years later, after Mom decided to sell her home to the guy who had once been our paperboy in his teens, the new owner, having known her for so many years, told her that she could take her time in moving out of the house. Big mistake! When she was still in the house a month later and showing no signs that she was ready to move, it was Aunt Tee and Uncle Miltie who drove up to Mount Vernon and literally kidnapped her with the intent of letting her stay with them until she could figure out her next move. It seemed like a good plan until Mom asked Miltie to stop and get her some cigarettes and when he did, she hopped out of the car, ran down the steps of the nearby subway and went straight back to the house. Eventually, my brother and her failing health convinced her to move to Washington, DC, but not before she procured two storage spaces for her things until such time when she would move into her own place. And as you might guess, that was never going to happen.

Going to college presented my mother and I with a new opportunity to bond. I had been accepted to Howard University and to Ithaca College in upstate New York where I was offered a scholarship. For my father, it was a "no brainer" because he believed that free money should be the deciding factor. So, when I explained that I had

had enough of attending majority Caucasian schools and wanted to attend my mother's alma mater, he reluctantly relented. I was already familiar with the Washington, DC area, having visited family there. My mother fully supported my desire to have a Black collegiate experience at the college that she had attended.

By this point in time, things at home had settled down quite a bit. My brother and I had accepted the fact that Mom would behave rationally for a while, but there would always be the possibility that something would trigger her and initiate a manic episode. As for me, I was more than ready to embrace independence and start living on my own. In my freshman year, I was assigned to Frazier Hall, the same dorm that Mom lived in when she went to Howard. I also had the advantage of having my homeboy from Mount Vernon attending Howard at the same time and he became my boyfriend. My mother adored him and often remarked that she held hopes that we would remain together and perhaps one day get married. But that idea quickly dissolved as he began picking fights with me

Shaking off the Dust

because he wanted to date other girls and was too chicken to be honest about it.

I immersed myself in my classes, but the lure of the college party life was strong, and it didn't help that my uncle owned a "juke joint" neighborhood bar within walking distance of the campus. By the end of my first semester, I was placed on academic probation because my GPA fell below the required 2.0. I had also gained a healthy interest in the political climate at Howard and was incensed, like many others, that the school, although touting itself as a premier historically Black university had no Afro-American studies department! Couple this with occasional visits from controversial leaders like Stokely Carmichael and H. Rap Brown and I found that I had a lot of distractions. During this time, my conversations with Mom revolved around staying focused on my studies and curtailing my social and political activities. But headstrong as I was, I thought I could handle it all and made little effort to make changes in my lifestyle.

By the middle of my second semester, I was still struggling

academically, but I thought it important to participate in a student takeover of the administration building to support the student movement for an Afro-American studies department. When I returned from the sit-in, I went straight to bed and was awakened by someone telling me I had a phone call. It was my father telling me in a very forceful tone that he had not sent me to college to participate in demonstrations and that if I did not buckle down, I could come home and find a job!

While I was ruminating on his stern lecture and still feeling that I had done the right thing, I heard that Martin Luther King Jr. had been assassinated. Due to the immediate outbreak of riots, as well as rising tensions on the Campus, they gave everyone passing grades in all their classes and they sent us home. It was the saving grace of my college career and allowed me to return the following semester on an even footing. I was determined to dig in and complete what I had started. When I learned that I would be graduating on time without so much as one summer school class, no one was more surprised than me.

It was awkward when my father insisted on bringing my stepmother to the graduation, but Mom handled it well and with aplomb. It was yet another example of her operating with grace under pressure and not allowing her state of mind to get the best of her or her situation.

By the time I was a senior at Howard, I had met the man who would become my husband. I had already decided that after graduation I would remain in DC and finding my future husband was enough to seal the deal. Things with Mom continued to remain calm after she almost lost her home, and I had come to accept several facts about her delicate mental state. First, I learned that her disorder was probably caused by a chemical imbalance in the brain, which could be corrected with medication, but of course this was not an option for her as she resisted taking medication. Second, without the benefit of drugs or therapy, it was likely the bi-polar episodes would continue for the rest of her life. And third, I was determined to live my life as best I could and tamp down the guilt I felt at not being able to do more for her. I understood that although we all face challenges, unless we want help or seek it, we are limited in what we can do for ourselves or for others.

When I became pregnant three years into my marriage, my husband and I got an opportunity to move to Atlanta. While I was excited at the prospect of starting a new life in a new city, I knew that Mom's issues would not go away.

But I thought if I could focus on my own life and my own goals, it would be better all around. About a month after I had my son Byron, Mom came for a visit. The first few days were delightful as Mom was very excited about the arrival of her first grandchild. Then one morning, I awoke to hear some muted conversation taking place in the living room. As the voices got louder, I got up to see what was going on. I intercepted Mom just as she was about to bring a stranger down the hallway to my bedroom!

She saw the look of panic on my face and tried to calm me down by assuring me that this man was a friend of hers she knew from Howard and that she was just planning to give him a peek at the new arrival. I knew full well that this was someone she had struck up a conversation with when she made an early morning run to the corner store to buy her first 40 oz. brew of the day. I politely told the man he had to go and then soundly lit into Mom about the inappropriateness of the situation, not to mention how reckless and dangerous it was to expose my newborn to a stranger's germs! While accepting my opinion, she feebly argued that indeed, she did know the man and that she simply wanted to give him a glimpse of her beautiful new grandbaby.

Relationships between mothers and daughters can often present challenges. We accumulate emotional dust as we mature and grow into adulthood, forging our own personalities and shaking off attachments to ideas, goals or habits that do not serve us. While we sometimes continue to look to our mothers for guidance and support, I found in my own life that the emotional dust of the constant presence of her illness was the clay that molded and shaped our relationship.

While she suffered from extreme mood swings and periods

of depression, I must also own up to frequently riding my own mental roller-coaster and experiencing periods of rage, depression, confusion and even indifference. I think what spared me additional mental anguish was the fervor I put into raising my son, my unending quest for a closer relationship with God and my determination to grab hold of the reins of my life and direct my own path. Raising children is never an easy job even in the best of conditions where there is a supportive partner and money is not an issue. Few of us live these ideal circumstances but we do the best we can. I never thought I would end up raising my son as a single parent and I'm certain that it was not a part of my mother's desired life plan.

Life with my mother was sometimes difficult, but I was always in awe of the way she faced adversity, got through it, and went on to live another day. How many of us have not had struggles regarding our mental health? It helps to have God in your life--to believe there's a Power greater than yourself that brings you through each day. I know that my mother had that belief and it sustained her through

95 years on this earthly plane. I am forever grateful for her presence in my life and for her impact on my journey.

3

THE CAREER THAT CHAOS BUILT

I cuddle up in bed with Mama, my body buzzing with joy.
It's our first night settling into a safe house in the heart
of Kingston, Jamaica, where we had fled to escape Leroy,
her abusive common-law husband. Mama's back faces me,
and she is quiet. I know I am to be quiet, too—a parade
of images flashes across my mind. I see Mr. Leroy, racing
home from his Lodge meeting, expecting the usual Sunday
feast Mama dutifully prepares for him especially succulent
roasted pork, gravy, and pigeon rice and peas. Instead,
he finds no savory aroma coming from the kitchen. He
screams Mama's name: "NORMA!" in disbelief that the
house is empty and there is no answer. A mattress on
the floor and a few empty pots and pans are all that greet
him in the darkened house. Maybe he wants to think it

is robbery, and we are at the neighbors' house for safety. But he is a street-smart man and realizes immediately that Mama actually had the gall to outsmart him—Mr. "Smarter-Than-Thou"—and fly the coop. Now, in the quiet of the safe house and the warmth of Mama's back, I want to giggle out loud so badly. We should be celebrating our freedom, but Mama is sad, so I can't show my glee. Anyway, tonight, I have Mama all to my 15 year-old self. I feel so good. We're unstuck from the muck and mire that has been our life for so many years. But, I wonder, how long will it last this time?

When I am asked why I became a social worker, I share harrowing stories from my childhood and teen years, like the escape from the nightmare that was our life with Mr. Leroy. There were numerous episodes of physical abuse, abandonment, and neglect, much of it by my adult family members, whom I liken to characters in horror, drama, mystery, and action movies. The roles of loving-kindness, laughter, or light were scant. Wanting to make meaning of chaos, to free myself from unhealthy emotions, and to offer myself in service to others led me on a mission to become a social worker.

Mama had a pattern of playing hide-and-go-seek in the lives of her five children, appearing and disappearing at will. I entered the world inside my maternal Grandma Ida's house in Manchester Parish, the house my great grandparents left her. In addition to the midwife, my mother's older brother was present, along with my 14 year-old aunt. Grandma named me Angella Vincentie, disregarding the name Beverly, which my parents had selected for me. Mama was 19, and I was her first child. My sister, Sharon, and brother, Nigel, were welcomed within the next four years. We all lived there together with Grandma until I was enrolled in infant school/ kindergarten. One week after I started school, Grandma shocked me with the news that Mama had left to live in Kingston. I was 5 years old and had ravenous questions about Mama's disappearance, but Grandma provided paltry answers.

Over the next two years, I bawled anytime Mama showed

up to visit us for a few days then disappeared into the night back to Kingston. On one of her pop-up visits, in particular, we were all comfortable in bed together—Sharon, Nigel, Mama, and me. I hugged her neck tightly and fell asleep. But, in the middle of the night, I felt her moving, so I grabbed her neck—maybe to the point of near strangulation—and she quietly lay back down. Imagine my surprise when I awoke the next day and discovered she had left me hugging a body double, a pillow. I bawled again until Grandma said unsympathetically in our native dialect/patois, "Angie, stap dat cow bawlin. Stap it!" I learned to cry in silence. And I knew it was best not to annoy my Grandma, who had a short fuse and would explode verbally at times towards anyone.

The wrath of Miss Ida was tested one night two months before my eighth birthday when I heard a baby crying outside our bedroom door, and it woke me up. Lo and behold, as Grandma would say, it was Mama and a baby. I jumped up, screaming excitedly, and was getting ready to let Mama and the baby inside when Grandma threatened,

"Angie if yuh evah touch dat door … Gwaan backa yuh bed, now." My 7 year-old hand went limp around the doorknob. Grandma was in her bedroom at the far end of the house, cursing at my poor mother, who is standing outside in the cool Manchester air, and begging to come in without avail. Grandma's voice grew louder and louder, "Mi nuh waan nuh mo gran pickney inna mi house." We, three children, were speechless. Eventually, the begging stopped, but Grandma continued on her tirade. The next day, we discovered Mama had a fourth child, my sister, Carole. The neighbors took them in. Mama was banished from our house. Grandma's husband, Mr. Emel, known in local dialect as Mas Emel, tried to intervene, and that made matters worse. Grandma ordered him out of the house, and though he returned eventually, as usual, Mama never returned.

The next time I saw Mama was a year later when I learned she had a fifth child, Peter. I was living in Kingston, the "concrete jungle", with Grandma's older sister, Aunty Evelyn. A better name for her would have been Lilith, as the female demon in the Bible who devours children.

It was Mama's fault that I landed in Kingston. I heard the whispers. Grandma felt angry and abused after Mama tried to place a fourth grandchild in her home. For that, we all paid a price. Being carried upstream in muddy waters against the current became my new life. Grandma, my consistent parent figure, left Jamaica for Canada to live with her son and his family. Before she left, I was shoved off, placed unaccompanied on a bus to move from the country to live in the city with a near stranger. No one knew my mother's whereabouts at the time. My siblings and I were separated, and I didn't know where they were.

Allman Town, where I lived in Kingston, was no comparison to the lush, bountiful countryside where Grandma, a retired schoolteacher, gardened, and Mas Emel was a farmer and butcher. The worst part about being plucked from the country was abandoning my own personal garden that Grandma and Mas Emel portioned off for me. I planted corn, sweet potatoes, yellow yam, and red peas. I never got the opportunity to watch my garden blossom.

In the city, I lived in a tenement yard—a large dwelling shared by five to six families. A wrought-iron fence surrounded the building and the limited concrete yard space that had two ackee trees. There I had no playmates, and I was forbidden from playing in the streets. Evelyn worked as a —helper/maid for rich White people in Barbican five days per week and sometimes on Sundays. I felt like a fish in a birdcage. Evelyn only agreed to have me live with her because my father, Clinton, whom I had only met once and remembered vaguely, lived in America and loyally paid child support. Mama shared this story one day during one of her pop-up visits when she took me downtown and bought me ice cream and an American apple from sidewalk vendors.

Evelyn was a consistent mistress of punishment because I became a bed wetter. She spanked me for —stinking up‖ her damn bed. I asked myself, "Why am I peeing in the bed? I am a 9-year-old girl." When I lived with Grandma, I did not wet the bed, and if I did, no harm was done.

SHAKING OFF THE DUST

Evelyn came up with a solution. She gathered a pile of old clothes and old bedding, spread it atop a suitcase, similar to a trunk made of hardened cardboard, for my makeshift bed. Just sleeping on the floor might have felt better as my body was longer than the suitcase. I continued to pee in the "bed" off and on, and the punishment escalated. Maybe I was unworthy and hopeless, this church-going lady concluded.

To add insult to injury, her niggard ways did not help. Some Saturdays, Evelyn would take me to Coronation Market/farmers market downtown. She stopped at her favorite bakery, where they served fresh long crusty buttered loaves of bread and scaled milk with brown sugar. This woman ordered for just one. I sat beside her and salivated while she enjoyed her treat. If I am lucky, a pinch of bread was offered but not one single drop of her milk. Oh, how I wished the hot milk would spill into her lap. In contrast, Grandma and Mas Emel were givers, and Mas Emel was like Santa Claus all year long. I started thinking, Mas Emel is probably living at the house while

Grandma is living in Canada. Maybe, just maybe, I could run away back to the country to live with him. But how will I get there? Plus, the last time I ran away, it did not go well for me.

Out of the blue one day, Mas Emel showed up at Evelyn's to visit me. It was magical. I snuggled next to him and whispered, "Mas Emel, mi nuh happy." He said tenderly that he would love to take to Manchester, but there was no woman in the home to take care of me. I am old enough to care for myself, I thought. I am already taking care of myself. Why can't he see that? Why? I have nowhere to go. What if Evelyn puts me out of her house? Then, I remembered how I hated when Grandma used to argue with Mas Emel about his drinking and sometimes would throw him out of her house.

"Yuh drink tuh much white rum, Emel. Mi waan yuh feh stap ar else," she threatened.

"Wat yuh mean, Ida? Why yuh soh miserable, ooman?" he fought back.

Before long, Grandma was throwing all his belongings outside on the red dirt and demanding him to "git outta mi house." We children watched in disbelief as he staggered away, empty-handed. Eventually, like clockwork, Mas Emel crept back; he and Grandma were laughing and talking, again; and he kept the treats flowing for us children. We mattered to Mas Emel. I wanted that feeling every day. It did not matter to us children that Mas Emel drank white rum every day, except the nights he stumbled home from the rum bar carrying no treats. The next day, in the daylight, we would go searching for the treats that fell out of his hands on the way home and salvaged what we could.

A few months after Mas Emel's visit, when I was 10 and in 4th grade, Evelyn moved to a better neighborhood called Kingston Garden because we were evicted. But now Mas Emel won't know where to find me, I lamented. It was Evelyn's one and only son's fault. He had done something to offend the landlady, Ms. Andrews. She even took me aside and told me about the offense and made me swear never to repeat it. So, I won't. Besides, I liked my cousin, who encouraged me to do well in school.

My school report cards showed that I was passing in all subjects, but the teacher raised concerns about my "daydreaming" during class time. When I lived with Grandma, daydreaming was not a problem, and I advanced easily from first to third grade. Evelyn, of course, spanked for not paying attention in class as if that could curb the daydreaming. It was true that I often got lost in my thoughts. I imagined reuniting with my siblings and living together peacefully with them in a big happy household where I would be in charge. The sting of the teacher's bamboo cane across my shoulder would shock me back into the classroom.

On Sundays when Evelyn had to work was ultimately my best days. She'd send me to church, and I seized the opportunity to go roaming the streets, go to by the wharf for peace and quiet, the perfect setting to daydream without incident. One fateful Sunday, tribulation fell upon me. A gang of girls rushed me out of nowhere. The biggest one admired my wristwatch, grabbed my arm, and began to remove it as I begged, "No! Please nuh tek mi watch, please mi ah beg yuh." The younger girls observed without saying anything as if they're watching a demonstration of how to steal watches.

Ripped from me was my most prized possession and a gift from my "faceless" father. The girls took off, and I clumsily ran behind them. They disappeared into an alley. I knew better than to venture any further and continued towards the wharf to search out a policeman. I found one who appeared disinterested in my plight. Feeling distraught, I marched up to the Central Police Station and pleaded my case. Thankfully, the officer agreed to help me. He ushered me into the back of a squad car and drove to the area. He went in the alley alone and captured the oldest gang member. She was wearing my wristwatch. I wanted him to snatch it off and give it back to me so I could go home before Evelyn returned from work. How was I going to explain my predicament to her? I expected no mercy.

The officer took us back to the station and made me watch while he chastised her. He commanded her to place all 10 fingers on the desk, took out a solid wooden stick from the desk drawer, and slammed it down on each finger as he repeatedly called her a thief: "Yuh too tief!" "Yuh, too, tief!" "Yuh, too, tief! ..." The girl yelped like an injured puppy. Fortunately, I was spared that Sunday night. The officer drove me home and did all the talking. The watch thief had a history of stealing, and he wanted Evelyn to pursue the case. She agreed, flashing a smile and revealing her gold tooth. It was refreshing to see her actually smile instead of bark at me.

Before my court date, Grandma had returned from Canada to escape the winter weather. She was impressed by my actions surrounding the robbery. Surely, I thought, she would take me back to Manchester even though I had become somewhat accustomed to city life. I wanted to escape Aunty. The answer was a flat, —No! — I felt doomed to a life with Evelyn.

As it turned out, the officer paved the way for me to get

praise. It came from my grand uncle, Nash, Grandma's brother. The recognition came after I had won my court case. Seventeen-year-old Sherrell Adams was found guilty of battery and theft and was sentenced to six months in jail. After my victory, I went back to Manchester to visit with Grandma. Nash, a gregarious businessman and bar owner in the same village, renamed me "deh Great Angella!" He told everyone about the robbery and court case. Everyone in the bar drank and toasted to that. I was beaming. I felt like the most important 11-year-old in the world.

Back in Kingston, I expanded my Sunday escapades, and my mother supported them. She gave me bus fare and invited me to secretly visit her on Sundays when Evelyn was at work. It took three buses from where I lived in Kingston to where she lived in St. Andrew. I often used some of the bus fare to buy a pound of sweeties at Lanneman's factory near my school. So, my transportation fund was sometimes short. Solution: I'd sneak money from Evelyn's purse, the one with extra cash that she kept underneath her bed. I did not give a damn. My life was miserable if I did well or poorly. I began to see that money could afford freedom and pleasure, and it wasn't as though I was sticking up anybody and robbing them as Sherrell did me, I reasoned.

Brazenly, I took the risky trek to enjoy time with Mama, and my two younger siblings, Carol and Peter. Leroy, her common-law husband, and father to my youngest brother Peter was not usually there. The less of him I saw, the better, I thought, as there was a part of me that did not take to Leroy. I could not explain it—my stomach would go into free fall while I was in his presence. I did not reveal it to Mama because I was too happy to be with her, and I loved that they owned a store. I imagined all the sweeties I could get every day if I lived there. My secret visitations successfully continued for well over one year. But Evelyn caught me for lying about nearly $2 missing from her purse. She started calling me "bad gal Angella," and I rolled with her insults.

One arbitrary Sunday afternoon, I was on the veranda

crocheting. (Evelyn had taught me how to keep my idle hands outside the devil's workshop, and I actually loved this craft.) Evelyn was in the communal kitchen cooking dinner when I saw Leroy's car pull up in front of the house. He had never been here before. I moved towards them cautiously and hugged Mama around the waist.

Evelyn appeared in the doorway, a surprised look on her face.

"Guh play!" Evelyn ordered and pointed at me. I barely moved away when an argument ensued.

I heard Evelyn talking loudly to Mama. And I heard Mama apologizing for taking immediate custody of me. And, just like that, I was freed from misery, or so I thought. I was 12-years-old and excited, yet apprehensive. I wished I could live with Mama and my siblings but not with Leroy. I felt conflicted but determined to make the best of my new home.

So, I was back to living in a single-family house that was located in a semi-rural community. The best part was that the house overlooked the Hope River. I shared a room and slept in a real bed with my sister Carol, who was 4-years-old, and Peter, who was 3. My other sister, Sharon, joined us a week later. She was 10 years old. (Nigel, who was then 8, had lived in the home, but Grandma took him back because he and Mr. Leroy could not get along, Mama said. I just knew something was amiss for Grandma to breakdown and take him back, but I kept my mouth shut.)

Life felt delightful. It was July, and school was out until September when I would start at Holy Trinity Junior High school. We would dress up, pile into the station wagon, and Mr. Leroy would drive us to their store where all kinds of grains and feed for farm animals were sold. They also sold groceries and sweeties and chewing gum. It was paradise. Below the store was an apartment, and Victor, Mr. Leroy's eldest son from his first marriage, lived there.

He was 17 and helped with the business.

When the customers came in, Mama proudly introduced me to everyone: "Dis ah mi big dawta, Angie," she said, hugging on me. I loved it. Going with them to the store daily was short-lived, however. Mr. Leroy decided we were old enough to stay at home. Mama agreed with him. I surely did not. I wondered, What the hell is the matter with her...maybe she rescued me from Evelyn to become a babysitter? Has my mother betrayed me? As usual, I had no voice. I was seen as a child, and children have a place which is "no place." Children should not be expected or forced to parent their siblings.

To make matters worse, I later discovered that Leroy attacked his son, Victor, with a ratchet knife the year before I moved in. Victor had an arm-length keloid scar to prove it. Both Mama and Leroy were "hush" about the mutilation Victor suffered at the hand of his father. It was incomprehensive to me. Oh God, I thought, his father is hundreds of times worse than Evelyn. I am living with Lucifer. Maybe he will cut me, or Mama, or my sisters and brothers. Did he cut Nigel? I must always be careful. I have to protect myself because I feel Mama won't. At this point, I had to admit the good in Evelyn and the best in Grandma. Evelyn never used a knife on me despite my "bad gal" ways. Grandma would only hit us children maybe twice per year with a leather belt she named "Doctor-Do-Good."

Immediately and secretly, I wrote to my father, in Bronx, New York, and pleaded with him to send for me … now! He wrote back, saying he was newly married, had a baby son, and was doing his best to get me there as soon as possible. I believed him, yet I wondered how long it would be before I could join him there.

Shortly, I realized my mother had "donated" her living brain to her tyrannical, alcoholic common-law husband. I knew in my heart if Leroy said: "Norma, let's kill de pickney dem," my own Mama would immediately begin digging three graves. My brother Peter, their golden child together, would be spared. I concluded this because she never protected Sharon and me from being brutalized.

Leroy busted our asses with all kinds of objects. Sometimes, Mama would beat us first "just because" he'd be the finisher. Once, when I was an 8th grader, Leroy cracked my head with a broomstick, causing my eye to swell closed for days. The school teacher saw it and sent me home. I needed medical attention, so Mama sent me to the medical clinic alone with a script: "Tell the doctor or the nurse that you were fighting with your brother and he hit you with a stone." Of course, I went off script in hopes of outside intervention, but all I received was an injection.

Furthermore, Leroy had a habit of calling Sharon and me "two big twin pussy gals" to degrade us. The verbal abuse started when I was only 13, and Sharon was 11. Mama began calling us the same thing whenever she was angry with us. To add confusion, when we were alone with Mama, she displayed kindness until her man walked in the door, and she plugged her brain back into his. Yes, my mother was a damn wuss! I vowed to never be like her. Actually, I didn't want to be like anyone in my family. I began fantasizing about actually taking down Mr. Leroy before he killed us. I had concrete, elaborate plans that included poison, but the get-away-with-it part was not clear.

In the meantime, I found another means of gratification. I began slipping money from the store and hid the loot in my panties. It was fair and proper compensation for forced labor: washing, cooking and cleaning; hauling water from the river; parenting; assisting in the store every day after school and every Saturday evening; and missing school days to labor on their chicken and pig farm, only to be rewarded with pummeling or whipping by "Mr. and Miss Massa." Many times, I'd share the loot, buying ice cream and treats for my siblings. Most of my money was spent on bus fare to school on the days Leroy would wake up before sunlight and command: "Nobody going to school today; your mother is sick, and you two (Sharon and I) have to help out." This would happen almost monthly when Mama had her monthly profuse menstrual cycle. I'd creep off to Holy Trinity, the only place where I felt safe and where I had a brilliant best friend, Annie Baker. Her friendship lightened my emotional load. If a lashing greeted me when I returned home, the next day, I would

74

compensate myself with more cash. When their drawer was short, and they could not account for the loss, they blamed each other for it. Mama mumbled that Leroy used it to buy liquor, and Leroy cursed Mama for giving customers items on credit and for being unable to collect. No fingers were pointed at me, and I doubt they believed I had the balls to "reward" myself. As it turned out, Mama slowly began to grow some balls of her own.

Miraculously it seemed, a guardian angel and mastermind, my maternal grandfather, Walter, swooped into Mama's life when I was 15 years old, and Mama was 34. It was ironic since he had abandoned Mama, his only child. He had lived in the Bronx, New York, for over 30 years, then retired and moved back home to Jamaica with his wife. Walter attempted to rewrite the script of Mama's life, demanding that she leave her "no-good" man for a better life. Naturally, he was met with resistance, initially at least. She agreed to let her father take custody of Sharon, who moved into their luxurious home in an upper-class community in St. Andrew Parish. (They also owned two rental houses in the Bronx.) I was happy for my sister, missed her tremendously, but I felt left behind.

At the same time, Leroy had closed the store, moved into the bush, and expanded his chicken and pig farm business. Getting to school became a daily undertaking. I had to leave home in pitch darkness, walk the three miles on a gravel road to the nearest bus stop, then take three buses to get to school tardy almost daily. With my energy drained, I would return home around sunset, ate dinner quickly, do a few chores, and then collapsed in bed. School became a blur, but I was determined to stay the course. Again, my best friend helped me stay sane.

Mama's generous side surfaced more often, and she'd slip me some money "just because," she said. Grateful, I saved some of it, used some for treats like Right On Magazine, and some for transportation to visit my grandfather sometimes on Saturdays. I would give him an earful about living with Leroy, the "terrorist." He would listen intently, but I couldn't read his stern poker face. He would always give me money on these visits. A few times, he summoned

76

Mama to his home through me. I'd partially eavesdrop as he lectured her, and Mama responded by crying most of the time. Walter said they were crocodile tears. I felt sympathy for her but wished she would follow his advice to free herself for a better life. It finally worked. Mama agreed to her father's well-crafted escape plan, of which I had the knowledge and was sworn to secrecy.

One Sunday morning, Leroy left for his Lodge meeting around 9 a.m. Two men appeared on the property around 9:30 as planned. Immediately and in silence, we all begin stuffing clothes, bedding and linen in pillowcases, slinging a few pots and pans into cardboard boxes, and turning over the mattress and dismantling the bed frame at heart-pounding speed. The men carried the bed about half a mile uphill first and rammed it into the truck, which was parked atop the hill. Then they returned to help us tote the remaining items. The agreement was to make a maximum of two trips in the allotted time. If Leroy turned back for any reason and caught us in the escape act, it would be our last day on earth. In a flash, Mama, my two younger siblings, and I were barreling towards Kingston and freedom in the get-away truck. But Mama had to make one stop. For our safety, she had to leave Peter with a family friend in Papine because Leroy had always threatened to kill her if she ever left the relationship and took their golden child. I was nervous Mama would not be able to give him up like she did her other four children years earlier. She did, however. We arrived at the safe house on the same day. Carole was placed with a relative, leaving Mama and me together. That day, I felt like the "Great Angella" again.

Unfortunately, freedom proved transient. We fled in July, and several weeks later, when I enrolled in Convent of Mercy Academy Alpha High School in September 1974, everything changed. Mama crawled back to Leroy, aborting the long-term plan to immigrate to Canada for the new start her father believed she needed. I had never felt so disappointed and full of rage—my blood boiling— towards another human being the way I felt towards my mother at that time. I shouted to Mama that I would check myself into an orphanage rather than return to the dungeon with them. She rejoined Leroy, so I closed my heart against Mama. Thank God, my grandfather, and his wife welcomed me into their home. I began to live in a peaceful and stable environment and was allowed to be a teenager socializing with friends from school and the Moravian Church the family attended. We enjoyed hiking and proud of my accomplishment in reaching the summit of Blue Mountain Peak—the highest mountain peak in Jamaica. But the new living arrangement was not without challenges.

My 68-year-old grandfather had multiple health challenges and carried guilt for abandoning Mama when she was a child. He told me he had retired in Jamaica, as opposed to his wife's preference for Florida, to establish a relationship with Mama and us. Later, I learned that his wife had a diagnosed mental illness. She said it was "melancholy," and she had been committed to Bellevue Psychiatric Hospital in New York for one year. Despite her idiosyncrasies, Walter adored her, and she did him as well.

When I was 17, my 70-year-old grandfather succumbed to prostate cancer and transitioned right before our eyes. I was relieved for two main reasons: He had been bedridden at home for one year, and we had to painfully watch his tall, well-built frame shrivel to bones wrapped in skin. Next, I was relieved of my "second-in-command" caregiver role. School remained a source of relief from the daily realities of my home life and, even though my grades suffered during the period of my grandfather's confinement, I enjoyed going. Moreover, I wanted to figure out a career path and needed a blueprint. Most of my school teachers were inspirational. However, Sisters Marie and Emma—two Filipina nuns—were my favorites. Both personified the essence of loving-kindness, grace, and unconditional love and, for a brief time, even entertained the idea of convent life. I terminated the thought because I enjoyed having a boyfriend and wanted to become a mother one day. Following graduation from high school, I enrolled in Alpha Commercial College to learn secretarial studies— practical skills to earn a living. I completed the 18-month lackluster program and began seeking employment. At the same time, I received my USA visa, the one my father had been working on for 8 long years, and a ticket to a better life abroad.

On June 24, 1979, I immigrated to New York to live with my father, his wife, and my 8-year-old brother. (Incidentally, I had met my father face-to-face for the second time the previous year when he visited Jamaica. At 19 years old, I was also introduced to the large, paternal side of my family and to my older sister, Mavis, for the first time.) There are hardly any words to describe the feeling of moving from a small Caribbean island to New York City. Still, overstimulating, overwhelming, overly exciting, and beyond expectations come to mind. Disappointedly, life with my father was far from easy, though we cared for each other. He, too, wanted to rewrite the script of my past 20 years.

We locked horns frequently -- I did not understand him, and he did not understand me. He said I was "hard to manage," which was true. Soon, he had enough of my "mouth" and told me to leave: "Angie, two bull caan reign inna one pen, one ah the bull hav' feh guh an' ah nuh mi, Pak yuh tings an' goooo!" He gave me one month to find my own place, and I did to his amazement. I had only been in the USA for approximately 18 months. He later claimed he didn't mean it and that he only said it to scare me straight. But, I had found a full-time clerical job that provided me sufficient income to support myself and pay for my college tuition. I enrolled full-time at Bronx Community College (BXCC) in the fall of 1981.

While at BXCC, I completed an introductory course in sociology, and it all clicked. I found my calling- social work. The fundamental role of a social worker is to assist individuals, families, or groups with issues brought on by abuse, neglect, domestic violence, psychiatric problems, and substance abuse. Social Workers identify strengths in every situation and build from there, so people can face challenges and deal with them more productively. I imagined how different my life could have been had a social worker intervened when I was a child and felt my mission was to save all others from suffering, especially innocent children. I also wanted to understand and rescue my mother. This was my genuine superwoman mindset at age 22. My ego was massive.

The journey towards my Social Work degree took many years, twists, and turns as with everything in life. For instance, I decided to become a single mother at 24 because I felt an inexplicable internal urgency in my gut to do it. However, working and parenting while attending school proved more challenging than I had anticipated. I don't recommend it. To become better at mothering than my mother, I deliberately put my daughter's needs first, and other people helped. I will be forever grateful to my village--family members and dedicated friends like Annemarie, Michele, Chester, and Joan, for their unwavering support. My daughter has grown up to become a brilliant and loving person.

By 1991, at age 31 years old, and two years after my 49year-old mother died, I earned my Bachelor of Arts Degree in Social Work from Herbert Lehman College. I was accepted into the accelerated Social Work Program at Fordham University, where I earned a master's degree in 1992. Afterward, I headed to Atlanta, Georgia, to be closer to nature, where homeownership proved feasible, and Georgia is a better environment for raising a child.

As a social worker, I have worked in diverse fields: child welfare, psychiatric care, medical care, and rape crisis. Through my training and professional experience, I have come to know that the muck and mire in my life had value because I put my rage and lessons learned from my chaotic upbringing to good use. I birthed a career necessary in helping others come to know their inherent value despite their circumstances. Though my younger self, superwoman, had set out with the belief that I could eradicate the suffering of others, I have come to know that this is impossible.

The world is not designed that way. And, there is no denying that my refusal to accept this truth had been a cause of unnecessary inner turmoil and distress. I had to shake off my unrealistic expectations. What's doable and responsible is my frequent practice of radical self-care while sharing my knowledge and experience with others. We all live in a world of duality where chaos and order must coexist. Both situations have value. Balance is the key.

4

An Unexpected Education

On March 25, 2016, I wrote in my Passion Planner that my goal for the next year was to, at least double my income and save the difference for retirement and, to write my book. Three months later, in June, I was offered a prestigious position that paid almost double my income – six figures and a title. I was incredulous, excited, and convinced that life had finally changed for the better! I was wrong.

The next year went from good to bad, to horrific! The new job was a horrible fit and, in the end, I felt like I had sold my soul for six figures. I thought God had intervened to give me that job, but before it was all over, I believed the Devil himself had set me up. I barely escaped alive.

And, once I did, my health was in decline, my self-esteem was eviscerated, and my hopes for the future felt bleak.

However, like many things that don't work out, it started great. But first, a little more about the job I had before I made the move to the high-paying, high-powered position. I was employed at a job that was good, but not challenging. It didn't pay anywhere near the salary it should have, given my experience and expertise. I accepted it because I needed to work. And, there were perks.

Every day I got to walk into a big spacious building, colorfully decorated with bright primary red, blue and yellow walls. I had a nice big corner cubby, filled with live plants and a huge window overlooking a tiny park filled with flowering trees. My brown, wooden desk had enough workspace for three people. I carefully arranged every knick-knack, and each one had a special meaning to me – especially my four-inch, imitation ivory Saint Clare, the patron saint of television. I found her at a gift shop in the Vatican. The ergonomics of my desk chair, which I got to pick out from an office supply catalog for the first time, supported my ample frame like a baby in a momma's lap. In the far corner of my cubby I had placed two modern, crisp red chairs. They were comfortable, balanced, and curved around your body like a hug. People would come around to say hello, plop in one of those red chairs and never want to leave.

It was a crazy mix of furniture from the production studios on the bottom floor of the massive building. You could pick and choose, with permission from the prop master.

I would always keep my essential oil diffuser going, and no one objected. I used lavender for calm, bright, pungent lemongrass for vitality and fragrant ylang-ylang to balance male and female hormones. My colleagues gravitated to my corner cubby, and I felt appreciated. Overall, life at the office was good.

Getting to that point had been a long, slow process. First, I worked as a contractor in a completely different role: on-air reporting on the legislative session. It's something I'm good at, and I enjoyed the mini celebrity that came with the job. Anytime you're on TV, people feel like they know you. They give you entrée to inner circles where you might not otherwise be welcomed.

When the legislative session was over, the contract ended. But, there was a full-time position as an assistant news director that I applied for. The competition was stiff, but I figured I had the upper hand since I had just finished the reporting gig. Three months later, I was hired.

The organization's culture was slow and deliberate. The intent was to allow for a thorough hiring process. On-boarding had a similarly leisurely pace. I was given three months to learn the terrain, settle in, and come up with a plan of action. I was assured by my boss, "We want to set you up for success."

During the hiring process, I was tasked with devising 30, 60, and 90-day plans. They became my operations manual, my blueprint. The investment of time paid dividends. I was able to learn the nuances of the position and the dynamics of the team. I had time to learn the lay of the land, get to know my colleagues and the young reporters I would supervise. I also got to know my boss better.

He had hired me months earlier for the contract reporter position with faith, far exceeding my own, that I could do the job. He was encouraging from the start, and let me know he believed in my abilities and talents. And his mentorship helped me live up to those expectations.

When he hired me for the first job of contract reporting, it had been years since I had been on the air -- reporting or anchoring. The passing years and added pounds, in an industry that idolizes youth and thin bodies, had sapped my confidence about being in front of the camera.

In fact, I almost sabotaged my interview for the reporter's job. I couldn't find anything to wear that looked attractive to me. I was on the brink of canceling, but my daughter, who had knowingly stopped by to "check" on me before I went to the interview, looked me in the eye and said, "I love you and everyone else will too." She said it with such faith and conviction; it gave me the courage to get past my nerves about my appearance and go to the interview.

The contract was only for five months, but it was one of

the best times in my journalism career. I got to report on stories far beyond daily politics. The best were the personal stories our team got to tell about everyday people, doing their jobs with little spotlight or attention.

Their common thread was a desire to preserve and improve democracy. I enjoyed the people I worked with, and until the last few months there, I had the best boss in the world.

He was intelligent, astute, and kind. He was a mentor in the real sense. He never lorded your failures over you but helped you to learn and grow from every situation. He was always the smartest guy in the room, but he never bragged and didn't have to. It was obvious. We talked every day. His guidance was gentle but firm and helped me build on my strengths as a leader.

That professional development time came to an end when he was promoted, and I got a new boss. You can usually tell when someone has preconceived notions about who you are and what you can do. But, in this case, it wasn't obvious – at first. I didn't pick up on the subtle clues that my new boss thought I was just a little less. Less than her, less than good, less than whatever. Just less.

That attitude started to show up as soon as she became my supervisor. Before that, there were sometimes little digs, but not outright condescension. There was the time I was required to "pitch" during a pledge drive. That's when public media asks listeners or viewers to donate, become members, or upgrade their memberships. I don't believe journalists should take part in pledge drives, but I did as asked. I had to pitch with her.

Pitching involves a fair amount of ad-libbing, which I can do pretty easily. It's a skill you attain as a broadcast journalist. She was very skilled at pitching but seemed incredulous that I was too. She repeatedly commented that she couldn't believe I was so good.

It was not a compliment. Once she became my supervisor, there was a condescending undertone to our conversation, and every aspect of what I did seemed to be under the microscope.

I could still confide in my previous boss and mentor. He always offered great advice and, more than a time or two, talked me off the ledge in my dealings with her.

His promotion left the news director position open. I was the assistant news director and of course wanted the promotion to the top spot in the newsroom. My mentor recommended me for the position. I wanted the job and was certainly equipped to do it. But the decision dragged on without explanation. And soon, my new boss was questioning my skills.

There was a particular story that I didn't edit well. I overlooked some key elements that should have been added. But when it was pointed out, I learned from it.

And that mistake didn't happen again.

However, that wasn't the end of the story. It was just the beginning of efforts to undermine my authority and effectiveness. It became clear I was not going to be promoted to news director.

We finally met over lunch so she could tell me about her plans. It was a strange meeting without a lot of details. I left with no clear understanding of what was next. She evaded all my direct questions, claiming she couldn't elaborate on anything because the plan was still under wraps. Some days later, she clarified.

She decided to restructure the news department. For me, that meant a lateral move. I would basically do the same job with a different title, but I would not be named news director. She was also going to take a more direct role in the operations of the newsroom. It would all be announced, she said, at an upcoming staff meeting. But before that could happen, fate stepped in.

I learned my name had been submitted by a colleague at the station as a candidate for the high-powered job at another organization. I talked to a consultant who was helping head up the executive search. After several conversations, he recommended me for the job. Things moved quickly. I had several conversations with their human resources staff. I was asked to apply for the job on-line and submit a resume. A few days later, I was asked to come in for an interview as the final candidates were being seen.

I called a cousin for advice. At the time, she was the head of human resources at a Fortune 500 company. I asked her how to approach the interview. She was amazed that I was on such a fast track. She told me it was highly unusual to bring in a new candidate at such a late stage in the process, "So," she said, "they must have been impressed."

I was excited and nervous, and a little scared. I was on the verge of seeing the manifestation of an affirmation I had made barely three months earlier (to double my income). This was also the first time I was ever interviewed for an executive position. It was heady!

I'd carefully picked out a pink and white suit-dress to wear to the interview. I felt great. Full credit goes to a dear friend, with an excellent eye for fashion, who guided me in the search for just the right look.

The interview was a whirlwind. I had to take a few tests to

show I could write a press release, figure out the ethics of a couple of hypothetical situations, and a few other things. After that, I was whisked into a huge conference room that would soon become very familiar.

There were five or six people, mostly women, seated on either side of an unusually long conference table. The "rules" were explained. They would each ask a question. I was to answer as succinctly as possible to allow them to get through as many questions as possible. And it was on!

It was my first panel interview, but oddly I wasn't nervous when I walked into the conference room. I stumbled for words a bit in the beginning, but after a few minutes, I just answered what I knew. I don't remember the specific questions, but they dealt with management style, knowledge of the media, and crisis communications.

After it was all over, I started second-guessing myself and thought maybe I didn't do that well. I went over the questions in my head and thought of answers that might have been better.

I thought, "This was a great experience," and figured it would go a long way toward preparing me for the next time such an opportunity came along. The next morning I almost hit my head jumping out of bed when I got a follow-up phone call asking if I could meet the next day for lunch with the man who would become my direct supervisor. Unequivocally, "Yes!"

I was so glad my friend, who helped me shop for the interview outfit, had the foresight to make sure I also got a couple of additional outfits. She sensed there would be follow-up interviews.

My supervisor-to-be and I met for lunch at a bright, colorful café. We talked about the job in detail and the idiosyncrasies of the big boss. We spoke about hypotheticals, management style, and ethics. We talked about the high turnover rate for that position and what a tough job it would be. And we also talked about rebuilding a team that had faced some challenges and instability. One of the most important things we discussed was mentoring. I was stepping into a field that was journalism-adjacent.

There were many areas that I was going to have to learn about and quickly.

To be a good reporter, you have to be a quick study. But when I need to learn something that I have no familiarity with, I like to take the time to study to gain a full understanding of the topic. But I soon learned there was no time for that.

The next step was to meet the team. We had lunch in one of the smaller department conference rooms. It was a bright, functional space with big windows that let in the sun, with a view of the nearby building tops. I was introduced to everyone and peppered with questions. We were feeling each other out – the team and I. In the end, it felt like a good fit. Then I was brought in to meet the "big boss."

I had been warned that she was not one to "suffer fools." I didn't know what to expect. She was a pretty woman with long dark hair, pulled back away from her face: younger looking than I expected, but no smile – just a steely gaze.

Sizing me up, she held my resume in her hand, with her elbow propped on the conference table. She let it drop dramatically to the table, as she said, with a half sneer on her face, "I see that you have awards for this and that. You even have a Peabody for coverage of the Gulf Oil Spill." "Now I know," she continued, "that you're not an expert on oil spills, so how did you come to learn enough about oil spills to win an award?"

"Oh," I replied, feeling a surge of confidence, "you want to know my process? I can tell you about my process." I went on to explain how I can totally immerse myself in a topic, figure out what I don't know and with whom I need to talk to find out. I have pretty good recall, and I'm able to process information quickly. It's a skill developed over many years of reporting.

She seemed to warm slightly to my answer. There were a few more questions. My supervisor-to-be stepped in to wrap things up. He was about to usher me back to the elevators to leave. He said the two of them would talk and get back with me, but the big boss said, "Why wait?"

and instructed him to have me meet the person who was leaving the job. She was a petite woman, immaculately dressed and coiffed. She smiled warmly and welcomed me into her spacious office. Her administrative assistant, efficient and organized, brought us cold bottled water and asked if we needed anything else.

We exchanged pleasantries and made small talk. She gave me an overview of the job. I asked her very pointed questions about why she was leaving. She told me it was primarily to return to working her own business, which she had put on hold while doing this job.

She offered a lot of great advice, but there was no way she could have prepared me for what was to come -- and the speed with which it would hit the fan. Still, she seemed a bit constrained. I understood why, after she mentioned that she had been carried out of that office on a stretcher. Later, several people would say it had happened twice.

Then she admitted it had actually been three times!

Stress!

But she must have done an excellent job because she was leaving in good standing and on her terms. The thought of being carried out on a stretcher was alarming, but I shrugged off the feeling of dis-ease it sent through me.

Surely, I would be able to negotiate the ups and downs of this job without feeling that much stress, I thought, naively. I was wrong.

I was heading home after meeting the team, the big boss, and myriad others when my cell phone rang. It was my supervisor-to-be. He said after careful consideration, he knew there were three things he wanted in the person who would be hired for the position: someone who knew the subject matter, knew how to work with the media and who had the right temperament. He said he knew he wouldn't be able to find someone who had all three qualities. I thought he was letting me down easy and about to tell me that they had decided to go with another candidate.

I zoned out a little, as I got ready for the let down when he said, "...so, we'd like to move forward and make you an offer." I was driving and had to pull over to keep from running off the road! I couldn't believe they had decided that quickly that I was the right person for the job!

This new position was definitely going to be a big step up. As I mentioned, it doubled my current salary, and it came with an executive title, a big office with a view, an administrative assistant, a team, and a budget of more than a million dollars. Excited does not begin to describe how I felt. I was overjoyed! And it was perfect timing -- just one more sign that God was moving my mountains!

During the interview process for the new job, things at my current job were deteriorating. There was more animosity between my new supervisor and me. We were always at odds.

I was just waiting for the formal job offer to come through before putting in my resignation.

I finally got it a day before my supervisor had scheduled a big meeting to announce the new structure for the department.

I can't pretend that I didn't find great satisfaction in being able to let her know, just minutes before the staff meeting, that I would not be a part of the reorganization plan.

I spoke with her privately before the staff meeting – and that changed the entire focus of the meeting. It became about my leaving for this new opportunity, rather than her decision to downgrade my role and responsibilities.

When you've been wronged and know God has your back, you understand that you may not be around to see "payback" or ""karma" kick in, but you know it will happen. However, when you're there to witness it, it's even sweeter. She had such a look of disbelief on her face. It was almost as if she couldn't believe that I had been hired for such a high-profile job. Oh well!

I wanted to give a full two-week notice, but my new employer had asked me to start sooner. I had quite a bit of vacation time built up and had previously scheduled a short girlfriend getaway to the beach with a friend. I cashed in the extra vacation time and was out of there within the next few days. My friend and I went to the beach for a couple of days and had a glorious time lying on the warm sand and soaking up the sun. I felt fortunate to be able to get in some downtime before starting my new job. It turned out that it would be one of the last opportunities I had for rest and relaxation.

Within days of getting back from the beach, the new job began. The first day was awesome! This was the first time in my career that I had an administrative assistant. I had to pinch myself. I had "arrived!" My assistant and the team had a catered luncheon to welcome me. It was some of the best barbeque ever! I was introduced to key people in the building, spent time getting to know the team, and had a chance to settle in. By day two, that all changed, and I understood why it was imperative to be proficient at crisis communications. A long-brewing crisis was coming to a head. And I was the lead on handling it. By day three, I was planning a major news conference.

I was the spokeswoman but knew very little about the situation. There were emergency meetings with department heads and key team members. A strategy was devised, and I thought we were all on one accord. But, oddly, my new supervisor said he wasn't ready to give the media all the information we had at the time. He wanted to wait for an additional report that wasn't crucial. He wanted me to ask reporters to hold their stories for a few days until we had everything in place.

"Not a good idea," I opined. "Reporters are not going to wait until you're ready. They're going to release what they have with or without your side of it," I warned. But, since I was just three days in, I was overruled.

The organization got through it, but unfortunately, the story had legs, a broadcasting term. It dragged on for days and weeks. Eventually, the facts showed that there was no wrongdoing, but the damage was done. Suspicions raised by the media lingered even when it was proven those suspicions were wrong. This new job was all about speed.

And, I had to hit the ground running!

The following week, I was asked to attend an industry

conference out of town with two of the senior team members. They had been to that conference many times and knew the lay of the land. It would be my first time at an event for this industry.

My administrative assistant handed me a thick, black binder. It was everything I needed to know about for that trip and the conference agenda. I looked forward to what I thought would be an opportunity to immerse myself in the new subject matter. It was perfect for the way I learn. I would have a week of immersion to help me understand and operate efficiently in my new role. The conference was jam-packed with sessions, and I was excited about soaking up knowledge from experts in the field.

But, I got a preview of how life was going to be in this new environment.

We had barely checked into the hotel when I got an urgent call. The big boss was trying to get an editorial published, and we had to shop it to the opinion writer at the local paper.

There was no time to unpack. We had to rewrite and edit the piece to the boss's satisfaction. She was rarely satisfied.

It took several hours of back and forth and a lot of wordsmithing from my colleague, but we were eventually able to submit the editorial and have it published. It was after midnight.

When I got my early morning wakeup call, I was excited about heading over to the conference site for the first sessions. Then I learned that my new supervisor planned to swoop in for the conference for a few days. He thought it would be the most effective use of time for us to split up and attend different sessions, then report back to each other on the content. He dictated which sessions, so my plans to go hear the speakers who I thought would help me learn the most were sidelined. In the end, it didn't matter much anyway. There was a crisis-a-minute underway back at the office.

I was ultimately pulled out of every session I attended by an urgent phone call, only to have to find a spot to open my laptop and get busy responding. I only made it through one complete session. Ironically, it was about crisis communications. I bought that book, which became my dog-eared bible. The conference experience set the tone for my tenure at the six-figure job.

There was a crisis brewing daily, and there was never enough time to actually do my job. I was always putting out fires – internally and externally. It quickly took a toll. Six weeks in, my new supervisor and —promised mentor‖ pulled me aside and said he didn't like the way I conducted a staff meeting. In fact, he said I should have canceled the meeting and dealt instead with one of the daily crises that were ongoing.

In my mind, it wasn't a crisis, and our team was addressing the issue. I thought it was essential to have that staff meeting. I had been hired, in part, to help restore morale. Team building is an important management strategy, and our weekly staff meeting was an opportunity to help build a tight-knit team. It would not be the last time my boss and I disagreed on a course of action.

It was clear mentoring was not going to happen, and I had to forge my alliances and figure things out. I dug in and studied. I worked a lot of long nights. I was on call 24/7.

It's ironic. In the end, I worked so many hours a day (and most weekends) that I would joke my six-figure job was probably closer to minimum wage when you added up the hours.

However, there were some good things. I managed a diverse team of highly creative people. That was a joy. It fueled my drive to keep going and keep trying. We had many successes as a team. Part of our role was to produce big events with hundreds or even thousands of people.

Many years earlier, I'd had a similar role at a non-profit where I had to oversee conventions and large gatherings. So, I had a passing familiarity with event planning. But, this was on a massive scale, on steroids. It's kind of like producing a play – you have to be a jack of all trades while maintaining control of the big picture. In the end, everyone breathes a sigh of relief and celebrates.

We were always in crisis mode. I mentioned many times that the organization did not have to be reactive to negative news coverage but could manage it by being proactive. There was an unnecessary fear of the media that drove many imprudent decisions. There were many times when negative consequences were self-inflicted. My media expertise helped me get the job. But when it came down to my advice, my boss often would do what he thought was best, whether it proved to be or not.

Our team marched on. We worked around the obstacles and managed to do some good work. We were finally gelling and functioning well together. I was eight months in and finally feeling confident about the job, until the night my boss called me back to the office, just as I was walking to my car following a late meeting. He met me in my office. We sat down at a table, and he told me that if things didn't drastically change, I would not be asked to stay in four months when the new fiscal year began.

He skipped over our team's wins during the previous months. He didn't say anything about how well the team was functioning now and how morale had improved exponentially.

He didn't mention how we had reached out to other departments to work with them and broken a years-old taboo of people coming to our department and interacting with our team.

He failed to mention the positive media coverage and much improved relations with the media that we had established since my hiring. He said my learning curve was taking longer than he anticipated.

"So, you're saying I'm not smart enough to do the job?" I asked.

"I didn't say that," he snapped.

"Yes, you did," I snapped back.

I reached around to my desk for a piece of paper and said, "Do you want my resignation?"

His eyes widened. "I will write it for you right now," I said, grabbing a pen.

"No, no!" he quickly spat out. "I didn't say that."

He told me I wasn't meeting his expectations, but oddly he could not and never did give me any specifics. With that new reality in mind, I doubled down on trying to make sure I understood exactly what he wanted. Mind you, we met every week for about an hour for what he called an "O3" or one-on-one meeting.

So, every week, we sat down and talked through goals and expectations. I kept running notes and was usually able to check off most of my to-do list. About a month after that conversation, there was an upper-level reorganization, and my boss was promoted.

The new chief of our department was someone I had worked with before. But our past relationship had gotten off to a rocky start. Therefore, I had made a point to apologize for any misunderstandings. Thank goodness, because now she was my boss. But, she also reported directly to my now former boss. I thought that meant that she would reverse the decision to let me go. She did not. At least not right away. She said she agreed with my former boss that I should not be asked to stay.

I was very disappointed and shared the news with the members of my team. They were disappointed as well and even lobbied on my behalf, which made me feel I'd accomplished what I needed to there.

I believe in being transparent. But, that was not the organization's culture. Some outside the department would whisper and talk in hushed tones when I came around. I would always let them know straight-up that I had been asked to leave in a few months. Some people found my honesty refreshing. But until I left, I was determined to continue doing the best job I could.

Apparently, it was a pretty good job. My new boss and I had to work closely, so I could hand off all the projects we were working on and provide detailed information for follow up. We also had to work on the ongoing day-to-day department needs.

Within a few weeks, she came to my office, closed the

door, and sat down. She told me that my former boss was simply wrong. She said she saw the value I brought to the department and didn't understand what the problem was. It was great to hear. We developed a close working relationship and completed several high-profile projects successfully

Yet, still, my former boss's decision stood, and I don't believe she was able to change his mind. As it drew closer to time for me to "resign or be fired," I prepared my resignation letter. There's an automated HR (Human Resource) process to resign, and once you "push the button" to start the process, it can't be reversed.

Just as I was about to push the button, my boss came and said she needed to talk to me.

She said she needed my help with an upcoming event and asked if I could stay until it was completed. I told her she caught me in the nick of time, and I agreed to remain.

That meant I would be there for another month or so.

The project was a bigger success than the year before, by all measures. We had a larger attendance, more sponsors, and more donations. Another production, done, and I was once again prepared to follow through with resigning. But once again, my boss came to me and said she needed me to stay. So twice now, I was being asked to remain on the job that my former boss inferred I wasn't smart enough to do. Again, I agreed to extend my time and said I could only work another few months until they were able to find a successor.

I eventually left the job four months after I had initially been asked to resign.

In the final days, it became awkward once the search was on for my replacement. It was past time to leave. I was drained and had given all I could. It took me a long time to get over the bitterness. I felt I had been misled, and promises had been broken. That job almost killed me!

My health declined because I didn't take care of myself. I didn't have time to work out. I went a whole year without

Zumba! My self-esteem was affected because even if you know, you're doing a good job, but your boss is continuously criticizing your performance, it can wear on even the most confident among us. My sense of wellbeing was shaken.

Right about this time, I had gotten a bad haircut. I wear my hair natural, and the stylist straightened it to trim it, but ended up chopping about four inches off, and not in a cute style. So, when I wet my hair right away, I knew it was bad. That bad haircut became symbolic of my recovery. I had to go to an expert stylist to re-cut my hair. Then I had to wait for it to grow out, which took about a year. That's also how long it took for me to feel healed from my experience at the six-figure job.

But that old saying, "What doesn't kill you makes you stronger," is correct. I learned how important self-care is. I learned to trust myself and my God-given gifts and abilities.

And, perhaps most importantly, I learned to speak up for

myself.

One thing my final boss at that job said to me was, "you should have advocated for yourself more." She was right, and I do that now.

It was a humbling experience, but one that's made me better. And despite the pain and mental trauma, I wouldn't change the experience. I've shaken it off with the dust.

5

Left To Tell: Life, Death and Rebirth

"Is she dead?" The voice came from one of the people who rushed to the overturned car.

Another person spoke through tears as she turned her head to avoid looking at the bloody scene. "Did someone call for an ambulance?"

"She must have been doing 80 miles an hour when the car hit that embankment," another voice spoke out. "Help me pull her from under the car. There's gasoline all over the place. It could explode. Careful."

I heard all their voices and watched from above as they worked to drag my broken body from the smashed ruins of the late-model Camry I had rented especially to take my sister and grandchildren to Dollywood and Gatlinburg, Tennessee late in the summer of 2007.

"I'm alive! I'm alive!" I screamed. "Can't you see me; I'm alive."

Then I realized they didn't see or hear me. How could they? I floated above them all as they placed my physical body far enough from the wreckage in case the car exploded in flames.

I looked down at my twisted, blood-spattered body, and yet I felt no pain. In fact, just the opposite. From my place above, I sensed enormous warmth and the most secure sensation I had ever experienced. Then I saw – no, I seemed to be enveloped by – a loving light that took me through a tunnel. At the far end, a bright glow beckoned for me to come deeper and deeper into the welcoming passageway. At the same time, I felt engulfed by an overwhelming unconditional love passing through me. It was so magical that my eyes filled with joyful tears.

I looked up and saw a rainbow with its arching colors stretched across the heavenly sky. A moment later, the smiling faces and cheerful sounds of my ancestors gathered among evergreens and maple trees that covered a lush green hillside.

Although I could not explain it, some celestial power told me I had come face-to-face with death.

Far from the grim scene of the accident, eternal healing and peace existed. My heart filled when I felt the inviting flutter of angelic wings beckoning me to come with them. They would escort me home.

From somewhere, a quiet, yet compelling voice whispered, "Come to me or go back. You choose." I believed it was God.

Even though I had no sense of the time I had to decide – for how do you measure time in eternity – I felt a sudden unbearable pain overtake me. My spirit had returned to my physical body as I lay in the grass where they placed me. My head throbbed in agony. It was torture to move my arms and legs. A searing heat engulfed my chest as I took a breath. And yet, I held onto the vision of my spirit floating above the people who came to meet and assist me through the passageway.

It appeared I had decided to return to what would soon be the prison of my earth life rather than remain in the dreamlike comfort of the afterlife. Apparently, I still had work to do here. My daughter, Demetria, my sons Robert, and William – all adults – and my eight grandchildren all still needed me. And I needed them.

As the eighth among the siblings in my family, most often, my opinion didn't count. They would tell me to shut up, sit down, and be quiet. Now, as a mother and grandmother, I get to choose, and I had unfinished business to complete.

But the pain that enveloped my body told me that important business would have to wait.

The next sound I heard was a woman's voice. "Let me through," she said."I'm a nurse. I can help."

I half opened my eyes and saw my Florence Nightingale push through the crowd. She knelt beside me, took my pulse while holding my hand. "Where's that ambulance," she bellowed. "You're going to be okay." I so wanted to believe her.

Through the commotion, I heard the shrill siren of the ambulance grow louder as it came closer. Moments later, doors slammed, and three men in white uniforms rushed to my side. They spoke in steady, overlapping voices: "Check her pulse." "Get gauze on that gash." "Bring the stretcher." "Hurry!"

All the while, the woman who said she was a nurse held a firm but gentle grip of my hand. I turned my head and risked another lightning bolt of pain as I looked at my hand in hers. Why did I take such joy to see the pink color of her skin blend with such softness against the rich ebony of mine? After all, this was still Atlanta. Some harsh beliefs about different cultures had lingered too long. But there was no division here. Not now. Even through the pain, I breathed a sigh of relief.

Strong arms lifted me onto the stretcher and strapped me in. "Make room," the man said. "Get the ambulance door open."

As the procession made its way to the ambulance, the nurse would not let go of my hand. It felt so reassuring.

This comforting moment allowed me a temporary escape from the pain. With an overlapping mixture of high hopes and deep concerns, I thought back to how this day-of-days began.

With only three and a half hours of sleep, I fought the urge to stay in bed. There was much to do, so I jumped into a cold shower. In addition to waking me up, the shower helped prepare me for the heat and humidity of another hot August day.

The night before, I had finished a grueling 450-mile drive from Dollywood to Murfreesboro, Tennessee to take my grandchildren home, and then home to Atlanta. I stopped only to gas up the car and grab quick meals – not my smartest decision. But we had been on vacation for a week, and now we were all anxious to get back home. The kids were filled with the excitement of a new school year. I was excited about a new position with a new builder and a new joint venture. My sister, though she loved the challenge of being with the kids, was ready to get home to some peace and quiet. Besides, I wanted to go to Sunday morning services at 7 a.m. That was important for the day I had ahead of me.

How could I not get excited about my new position and the possibility of increasing my salary to over $150,000 a year? Other agents working with this builder were topping $200,000 a year, so busy that their commission checks sat in the trunks of their cars because there was no time for small matters like going to the bank. Adding to my overloaded schedule on that fateful Sunday, I was to meet with my real estate friend and soon to be partner, Joyce, about our joint venture to purchase an herb franchise.

As a student of naturopathic medicine, I'd done extensive research and study on the healing effect of herbs, and we believed there was an increasingly growing market for them. We knew it would take serious financial risks to get it off the ground, but if it worked the way we planned, we could double our current incomes in less than two years.

Making more money had always been a driving force within me. I patterned myself after my dad and my brothers, who had been prominent attorneys and astute businessmen. And as driven as I was to earn and have more, I also knew in my heart, there was more to having a successful life than a bigger house, pelted furs, and $12,000 chandeliers.

Anyone who knew me knew I was willing to work hard to accomplish my goals. But I struggled to find the balance between achieving fleeting corporate rewards and recognition and maintaining a healthy personal life with my family and grandchildren. They were growing older and needed more of my time. The lessons and values I learned from my parents and the teachings from my church helped me weave through this struggle.

When my pastor gave her sermon that Sunday of the accident, I felt she had prepared her inspiring remarks just for me. Her words describing the "oneness of the universe" made me feel whole and complete, a part of a magnificent whole. "We are one with the omnipotent power," she said, ending with, "I live that you live."

I left the church with a feeling of serenity and well-being, which allowed me, at least for the time, to be at peace with the devastating news that previously seemed to overwhelm me. I was carrying a heavy load.

First off, my daughter, Demetria, had just learned she had breast cancer. Two months earlier my sister Janice, had been diagnosed with Transverse Myelitis, which is an autoimmune disease that causes inflammation of the spinal cord, severe pain, and loss of movement in the body leading to paralysis. While doctors can help reduce the pain, the rare disease is still thought to be incurable.

It is said that "trouble comes in threes." Mine did. My brother, Lamar experienced a life-threatening hemorrhagic stroke. He lost his balance and fell down the escalator at a MARTA station. Many people die from the bleeding in the brain within a few days. Since he survived, his doctors seemed optimistic that he would recover. But, they said, it would be difficult, and the hemorrhaging could reappear.

Still, I was running on adrenalin from the church service and decided to treat myself to a shopping spree at Fry's Electronics to purchase a laptop computer since it was a tax-free weekend.

Before I realized it, the afternoon had slipped by, and I needed to rush home for my 5 p.m. conference call with my new sales manager. He wanted to give me all the details of the new sales center and model home. Both of us were so excited, and we couldn't wait until Monday morning to talk.

I hurried through Atlanta highway traffic, weaving around cars, cutting some off too close. I was approaching my turn and raced onto the straightaway leading to it. I rounded the curve that leads to my neighborhood, and a half-mile from the entrance to my subdivision, all my pent-up energy gave way. I dozed off, falling into a deep sleep.

In my next waking moment, I realized I was pinned under

my car. Later I learned how I got there. While asleep, I must have stepped hard on the gas pedal. The car picked up speed and careened across several neighbors' yards, knocking over trees, and bulldozing small bushes.

Workers were installing a drainpipe to run along a ditch in one of my neighbors' yard. They had piled up dirt, which created an embankment that acted as a ramp. My car hit it, moving at racing speed. As if it were a circus show, the car soared into the air, flew over the ditch with such a force that it scaled a twelve-foot telegraph wire and dangled in the wires between two telephone poles. The wires stopped the forward movement of the car before it crashed to the ground. Even though I wore a seat belt and the airbag inflated, I became twisted in the wreckage when the car fell.

How I survived is a miracle.

More important is how I visited the hypnotic illusion of death and returned to bear witness to some of life's mysteries, blessings, and age-old lessons.

The miracle of my survival started with those brave and selfless souls who came to my rescue. And to those who transported me and cared for me during my journey in the hospital.

It is amazing to me that the EMT's, who are so proficient in emergency response, seem to know where every pothole, depression, and bump is in the street on their way to a trauma facility. I had to endure the pain of that ride because when a person experiences certain types of injuries, the EMTs are restricted from administering certain drugs. They want the patient to be awake to provide as much information as possible regarding what happened, pain location, medical history, current meds, and other pertinent information.

As I awaited the results of my x-rays, MRI, ultrasounds, and blood tests, I noticed I was annoyed that the EMTs literally destroyed my favorite dress.

They actually took surgical scissors and cut my black linen Ann Taylor straight down the middle, and off my body!

To this day, I never found out who made it to the hospital first, the ambulance, or my family and friends. All I know is that when I came to, those I hold dear were standing around my bed, eyes glaring, looking scared, and trying to repress their own alarm. They took turns telling old lame jokes that forced everyone to laugh heartily until laughter became the joke.

Mine is a family of singers, and my maternal grandmother could pray to raise the clouds off Atlanta. So, as they stood around me, they sang, and I tried to sing with them. At one point, we became so desperate for joy, we sang "—Joy, Joy, Down in Our Hearts," followed by "Jingle Bells" in the heat of an August day. Where love prevails, any good thing can happen.

At last, the doctors came in with the test results and relieved all of us. We had lamented long enough. Once they had gotten my permission, based on HIPAA regulations, the doctors could give me the results in front of the group. We were told I would need a five-hour, open-back surgery, during which the surgeons would go into my left side, collapse my left lung, and move my organs around to allow space to infuse titanium plates and screws at three points along my spine. They might need to use my last rib – the floating one, which was pretty messed up in the accident. They figured I wouldn't need it anymore, and they could use it to help stabilize my spine. This would be considered an emergency surgery, given that I could turn my body the wrong way and be paralyzed or crippled the remainder of my life. The success of the surgery was not guaranteed, the doctors cautioned.

The pain medicine I was given earlier for my back had started to take possession of my mind and body. These people who would ultimately be taking care of me were beginning to look blurry, and their voices seemed to echo from another room. Who told anybody it was okay to give me Oxycontin? The drugs had a hold on me. It appeared that people were sitting in the middle of my room with a hot steaming serving table. The haze from the steam had filled the room; it was so heavy I could barely see in front of me. A voice from behind me kept saying, "Potatoes or rice?" "Are you having - potatoes or rice?"

I remained in the hospital from that infamous Sunday on August 5th until the end of the month. Knowing the director of pharmacology, an anesthesiologist, and two phlebotomists who worked that trauma facility was of great comfort.

My family had the warriors on the case, researching the history and background of the medical team. I was determined: No one was touching me until I found out if they prayed. I told the surgeon, as far as I was concerned, we were like ships passing through the night. He didn't know me nor me him. Now, this catastrophic event had brought us together. I had read all of his credentials and knew him to be "one of the best neurosurgeons in the country." "But do you pray?" I wanted to know. It was not enough that he believed in prayer. The question was, "Do you pray?" He shared with me that every time he goes to the sink to wash his hands before surgery, he looks in the mirror and prays. He said he prays for the success of the surgery and the healthy outcome of his patient. I was perfectly satisfied with a praying doctor with top-notch medical credentials.

Meanwhile, the drugs were not killing the pain. They were anesthetizing my brain. This time the steam table had taken on legs like stilts. It was moving from the cafeteria, passing through my room, on its way to the meadows. I was losing a grip on reality.

While I remained in that drug-induced, semi-conscious state, I could sing, but I couldn't pray. I could only sing to the lullaby, "Jesus Loves Me, This, I know."

I did, however, give thanks for my minister, family and friends, the intercessors, my naturopathic medicine classmates, doctors, and ambassadors. It was the magnificence of all this work in practice that helped to sustain me, and eventually, get me off the drugs. The patients and staff on the floor that I was on had heard and seen the good results of visitors who brought flowers and lifted the spirits of other patients. But they had never witnessed what was going on in my room, and they wanted to know more about it. A steady stream of friends, many with knowledge of spiritual truths and various forms of healing arts, took turns and stood vigil in my room every night. They would sleep on a pull-out chair that converted to a bed of sorts. Someone was with me until they felt it was okay to leave me in the hospital alone.

The hospital was a teaching hospital, and the student interns would make their rounds in the mornings accompanied by a resident. One morning a young intern performed what I thought was "the drill." "Did you feel that?" he asked. "Of course," I responded. "That's interesting,"he said, too stern for his size and stature. "Oh," I retaliated! "Yes," he said, "because I didn't touch you." I was busted. At that moment, no matter what my ego had going on about doctors and traditional medicine, it was clear that I had a great team of medical professionals caring for me. At the same time, I had enough faith to know with certainty that I got to choose whether I would walk or not. I set my mind to make my parents' teachings right: I would "pick up my bed and walk." I had already received my healing as I floated to that hillside among the evergreens and maple trees where I had met my ancestors and saw the face of God.

The doctors were encouraging in their comments about how the condition of my body contributed to the success of my surgery. The blessings of good muscle tone and a proper diet that I carried into surgery resulted from a 26mile marathon I had completed in Kona, Hawaii, to support the American Heart and Stroke Association. I had long tried to stay active, zip-lining 200 feet and rappelling from the top of the Catskill Mountains, and walking 60 miles in the 3-Day Breast Cancer Walk in years past.

Although the marathon was for an excellent cause, I was more focused on the physical challenge and the chance to earn a medal for completing it. God soon revealed a greater purpose and vision for my participation. As I trained, somewhere around the six-mile loop of Stone Mountain Park, the Chattahoochee River trail, and the Cooper River Trail, it became apparent that God wanted me to focus on the goal of raising research dollars to help end heart disease and the threat of debilitating stroke on women, men and children. The $5,000 each more than 2,000 runners had to raise to enter the race could make a significant impact in battling the disease. That vision made me even more committed to the race.

And even though I had begun to feel tired and two blistery masses were growing underneath my right foot, heel and sole, I crossed that finish line. Looking back on that victory, I thought, If I could win that race, surely I could rise-up like the great Phoenix from the ashes and win this one. Lying on the gurney and looking out the window of the transportation vehicle that took me home from the hospital, I felt a sense of victory. After almost a month in the hospital, I was finally going home. I was thinking of the inner turmoil I experienced day-to-day, struggling with how to stay alive. That was coupled with this very insistent full body cast I would have to wear for six months, squeezing and tugging at my skin. The discomfort of it was draining the very life-breath out of me. I looked like a mummy hungover from the dynasties of Egypt. The

SHAKING OFF THE DUST

prosthetist insisted that he had taken my measurements accurately, but it certainly didn't feel that way.

As we rode, gentle tears streamed down my cheeks as I'd lost count of my many blessings. My wonderful adult children, whom I loved dearly, handled the business side of my hospital stay, including the bill and insurance. The daily mounting costs were astronomical. I could just hear my daughter asking to have every iota of the bill analyzed, dissecting the charge of the ―tube within the tube,‖ the cost of the drugs, and every detail.

There wasn't much I could complain about; I had an enormous sense of gratitude for being alive.

The transport vehicle pulled into my driveway with a light thump, and I had my first indication of pain since leaving the hospital. I was so engrossed in my thoughts and reminisces that I was not focused on pain. This goes to show that where the mind goes, the energy flows. I was excited to see how beautifully the lawn was manicured. And my hibiscus garden was showing masses of colorful blooms. My neighbors were standing on the front lawn, anxious to welcome me home and help my sister and brother into the house and out of the sweltering summer heat. I'd missed our early morning runs, coffee clutches over designing our vision boards, sharing the new blooms of our flower gardens, and all the many things that you share as neighbors. I'd had fears and nightmares about whether my friends would pull away from me now that I had all these medical issues and faced a long convalescence.

Once I'd settled into my downstairs library, which was subbing for a bedroom until I learned to climb steps again, I could really exhale. My daughter and sister had arranged 24-hour care for me. My sister Jackie, who is very compartmentalized, had drafted a chart that had the names and days that people had committed to caregiving. And at night, I had a registered nurse. Every area of my life was represented among those who were committed to caregiving, real estate, church, naturopaths, spiritualists, neighbors, grandchildren, children, siblings, and friends. For months, they showed up like experts skilled and trained in their professions. I had physical and occupational therapists on alternate days to teach me to use my body again, and do things that previously were simple, but now seemed virtually impossible, like roll my body from side to side and lift myself up. It took weeks to accomplish those goals as I pushed through the pain to the point of exhaustion and tears. I give thanks for those dedicated, tough-love therapists, without whom I might never have gotten off my seat and on my feet again.

Nobody mentioned the ugly face of unrelenting pain when I left the hospital. Nobody wants to discuss the possibility of prescription drug addiction that might go along with the recovery process. I was naïve to think I only had to go home and meditate, stay hydrated, reconnect with the use of my body, stay in motion, and stay in prayer. I had prayers from religions I'd studied from all over the world, and my global friends shared indigenous prayers and results-oriented practices used by their ancestors for healing. My most fervent prayers during those days were to be able to come off the drugs, which were causing anxiety. Then another drug was given to cope with the anxieties.

The "new" pain, I called it, resulted from nerves and muscles severed during the surgery, trying to reconnect and find their pathways back home. The nerve and muscle endings were literally tearing across my back to reconnect. No amount of medicine can anesthetize that pain. What I discovered that prescribed pain medicines do, however, is dull the brain, so it doesn't feel any pain. I became lost in a mental and emotional fog and felt fatigued and physically incapacitated. I would start to meditate or open my mouth to pray and trail off to nowhere land instead. I was beginning to feel spiritually bushwhacked.

Breaking through the darkness and loneliness of my own sleeping consciousness was one of the hardest aspects of my recovery. As a result of the trauma of the accident, I was diagnosed with PTSD. The doctor had changed my prescriptions many times to variations of the same medicines with different dosages, to no avail. Even then, I was convinced the medications may be the culprit.

Out of sheer desperation, my daughter took me to get mental health assistance. We talked with a professional pain management specialist who advocated "staying in front of the pain." That meant, "Continue taking your medicines as prescribed and don't get off the schedule because you don't like how the medicine makes you feel." As someone who does not drink alcoholic beverages, have no medicine cabinets in the house, or even keep aspirin on hand, sticking to a regimen of pain medicines took a disastrous toll. The therapist was extraordinary in her counsel, and I could feel her good intentions as we set goals for me to have better mental functioning. Her program required me to be seen by a psychiatrist who evaluated my medical history and recommended Zoloft. I was already at the all-time lowest ebb of my life, and the mention of Zoloft woke me up fast. The one thing I knew for sure was that I was not about to take any Zoloft. The psychiatrist became outraged at my refusal to take the medicine. He hit his desk with his fist, threw a fully executed temper tantrum, and screamed, causing my chest to pound like a herd of fiercely galloping horses on their way to nowhere.

"Why did you come to see me if you're not going to follow my advice," he asked angrily. I explained respectfully that I came for counseling, not Zoloft, not another drug. The doctor all but threw my daughter and me out of his office.

My challenge with the medications was happening around the same time the actor playing the lead role in the movie "The Dark Knight" took an overdose. He was on a myriad of prescribed opioids, which resulted in his death, according to news reports. This country has seen an epidemic of deaths due to the overdose of opioids in recent years. There are currently billions of dollars in lawsuits against opioid manufacturers, according to the Department of Justice.

The great outcome from my mental health excursion was that I went home and collected all my prescribed medicines, poured the pills into a paper bag with water, wrapped them in plastic, and threw them in the trash.

I wanted to flush them down the commode, but my daughter's environmental antennas went way up. She had real concerns about the drugs releasing into the water system and possibly doing harm.

Once the drugs were gone, I had space to breathe within my body, and I could think more clearly. I could walk the floors of my house without feeling that my feet and legs were sinking through the hardwood and the concrete, to the foundation, and to the ground. I could start anticipating a truly healthy, nontoxic recovery. I went out into the back yard to the security of the big rock that I sometimes called "my big brain." As I'd done many times before, I climbed up on that rock and watched the sky. At night I could reach up, and the stars felt low enough to embrace. It was my place of meditation and comfort, freedom from boundaries, and constraints.

Upon descending from my big brain, I called a trusted doctor and teacher to talk and schedule an appointment for acupuncture treatment. It had been so long since I had experienced the freedom from the pain the acupuncturist's needles produce. They treated the intercostal muscles between my 12th and 13th vertebra. That was accompanied by a good dose of myofascial release work to the free restrictions to connective tissue, which eased the pain and restored motion in my body. I felt totally inspired. That night I took my first dose of organic bromelain and Boswellia to eliminate pain and inflammation. Then I heated up the Crockpot for a concoction of bone broth soup, which would be ready within the next 48 hours if I was lucky. I pulled out some books and research papers from my holistic theology program and settled down to a cozy night of reading. I woke up feeling alive and refreshed after having the best night's sleep that I'd had in two years.

I did not get off prescribed drugs of my own volition, even though it was my prayer and heart's desire. It was a myriad of practices with my inner circle of friends and supporters. I created vision boards with the sisterhood and friends, scripted with family, prayed with my ministers and intercessors, tapped with dedicated emotional freedom technique practitioners, and did chi gong with my teacher and guru.

Being mindful of the holistic approach to my health and well-being made me feel new in mind, body, and spirit. The body has the propensity to heal itself. It needs certain mindfulness to support the process, which does not occur in a vacuum. It occurs in a field of love, light, and like-mindedness with other people to nurture and mirror the healing process.

Just as I thought I'd figured it all out, life gave me one more opportunity to learn lessons of gratitude and forgiveness, another chance to gain deeper understanding and wisdom. About six months after the accident, my spiritual sister and I revisited the site of the accident one Sunday evening. I hoped to get some additional insight into why the accident happened - why I was literally snatched out of my body and survived a near-death experience?

I studied the ground, looking for clues, listening, picking up rocks and stones. As I did so, I remembered the day before the accident.

We were driving from Dollywood in Knoxville back to Murfreesboro and stopped for gas at a station that had a little park site with beautiful begonias and pansies, picnic tables, and a small walking trail. My grandchildren and I helped my sister get situated from her walker to a bench before we took off exploring. We stretched our bodies and then strolled a distance, not going far from my sister's sight. Soon, one of the kids called out that they'd found an interesting piece of fossil. It turned out to be a stone wrapped in a piece of sedimentary rock, just waiting to be found. It was an exciting moment for all of us. Our interest in stones and rock formations had been passed down through several generations by my maternal grandmother. I told my grandchildren the story of how stones evolved to become a natural attraction for our family. They loved to hear stories of what they called "the olden days." I explained that my grandmother would share how her love of stones and rock resulted from how the early slaves used them to mark trails along the various routes to take them

SHAKING OFF THE DUST

north to freedom.

Suddenly, I was jarred back from reminiscing about that day of stone collecting with the grandchildren, to the present moment by the sound of a car racing its motor to get my attention. I was standing in the middle of the road. As the car passed by, I noticed a small, brownish grey rock on the ground at my right foot. I picked it up.

This little rock in my hand reminded me of the big brain rock in my back yard that I had requested the contractors leave when I was building my house. It was an important touchstone for my family and me. Many lessons were learned on top of that rock. My grandchildren had learned to read chapter books sitting there. And many morning coffees and meditations happened on top of the rock, not to mention evening prayers whispered in the sunset. When I found a stone that was a replica of the big brain rock near the site of my accident, I knew this was a sign that the accident was a source of healing and rebirth.

As time passed since the accident, I could sense I was

letting go of the pain, grief, and anger the accident caused. Some days I'd be angry, locked into a touch, smell, or sound that reminded me of the dark days following the accident. But most days, I was simply so happy to be alive. I had learned the real purpose of my life. All the years I spent building a professional career, chasing one more lucrative opportunity after another or one more chance for recognition and honor paled in comparison to the riches I had in the gift of my family and friends who shared unconditionally of themselves.

As I unleashed my judgments and opened myself up for loving people for who they were and not who I wanted them to be, the pain in my back eased to a measurable extent. At that point, I could begin to see the psychological and emotional ramifications of my thoughts

on the pain in my body. I had finally overcome and shook off the dust of that horrific accident and the persistent pain I allowed it to cause in my life starting on that hot August Sunday.

There's beauty that's come with the revelation that I no longer have to chase after life and that my health and friends and family that love me, and that I love immeasurably, are my most valuable assets. All the money in the world can't buy these things. I am dwelling in the wisdom that turned my values around and gave me the growth to shake off the dust. Now I can sit underneath the Bodhi tree and let the world come to me.

Coda:

And when at last it came to pass

I too have washed my hands of it

Time shall be no more As final thoughts be cast

Unto the winds they soar!

6

JACKRABBITS DON'T DRIVE CARS

Jackrabbits don't drive cars. At fourteen years of age, my grandmother prophesied that when I had babies, Jackrabbits would be driving cars. I saw the image in my mind and thought her words funny. This was long before the pink Energizer bunny was selling batteries on television. Those words would later pierce my heart. I asked why she felt that I would never have children. She told me it was because I loved babies too much. This was a part of her theory that you were never to love anything more than you loved God or what you loved would be taken away. This philosophy may have come from her losing much of what she loved at an early age. But she was right.

I loved babies. The first real baby I loved was my baby sister. I was four when I held her not long after she was born. She was tiny, about the same size as one of my dolls. She could do everything I wanted my play babies to do. I was also the girl in church who always wanted to hold any baby that came through the door. I loved the smell of baby oil, the touch of the baby's skin, and the sound of their giggles and coos. I loved to tickle their cheeks to see them smile. I held each baby as I had held the dolls that were frequently nestled under my Christmas tree each year. As a child, I was always planning my future, and I dreamed of being married and having six children, other times four, finally, I settled on having three. I thought three was the magic number. I wanted two girls and one boy, just as my mom had. Although I dreamed of being a mother, I was in no rush. I wanted to have my children the old-fashioned way - in the covenant of marriage. And no other way would have been acceptable to my grandparents. My grandfather warned of my impending doom if I were to become pregnant while living in his home; he said, "I will shoot you dead as you got to die." Those were his exact words. I took his admonition seriously. I had heard stories of how he forced my aunt away from home with a shotgun and a few choice words when he learned that she was pregnant as a teenager. Perhaps, my grandmother's rabbit was a reference to the initial pregnancy test that used a rabbit to predict pregnancy as a warning against my becoming a teen mother.

In my mid-thirties, my dream of having babies was shattered along with my idea of creating the perfect family. Mother's Day reminds me of my life's dream that never came true. I celebrate the beautiful mothers in my life, but it saddens me that I haven't had the experience of getting pregnant or giving birth to a child. My journey with reproductive health issues began when I was in high school. I often had periods that would last for weeks, only ending with an injection from a doctor. Later, two surgeries to remove fibroid tumors and an ovarian cyst left me unable to get pregnant. When I share my stories with others, I am often told that there are babies just waiting for a home and that I would make a wonderful and caring mother to one of the thousands of children in foster care. These thoughts do cross my mind, but perhaps my wanting children had more to do with my idea of creating the perfect family more so than it did parenting. I wanted a family that shared the same bloodline, a shared history, and an anticipated future.

As a child, the perfect family looked like the ones I saw on television, just shades darker. I loved *Leave It to Beaver* and *The Brady Bunch*. These families came into my home each week. I was fascinated with their stories and their family dynamics. They lived in homes where there were a mother, father, and children. Their homes were immaculate. The mother wore beautiful dresses and spent most of her day preparing for her husband to come home after a day at the office. For dinner each evening, they ate a delicious meal at a table where everyone sat and shared the highlights of the day. There were lively conversations and lots of laughter. Beaver was often chastised for his mischief but never spanked or beaten. The Brady bunch was a blended family that was always there to support each other. These families were in contrast to my families.

I had two. One of my families consisted of my elderly grandparents and me.

I was born in Washington, DC. and was brought to my grandparents' home in rural Georgia to visit by one of my mother's older sisters. It was there I fell in love with my grandmother. She was a traditional grandmother who baked cookies, churned homemade ice cream, and was very loving. When my aunt loaded up her three kids in her black Ford Fairlane to return to DC, I was left behind. I thought it was my choice. Before my aunt had driven away, my grandmother, with her kind, sweet voice, began to cry what I know now were crocodile tears. She said, "Everyone is leaving, and I'm going to be all alone. I wish I had just one grandchild to stay with me." I looked in her eyes and said, "Grandma, I'll stay." Just by saying that I felt that I had won the grandest prize, the pleasure of staying with my grandmother. I was happy until I realized that my aunt and my cousins were gone and not coming back. I never asked my aunt, mother, or grandmother why I was left behind that day. Looking back at that time, I

SHAKING OFF THE DUST

realize there was a conspiracy, and my mother and I were in the center of it. My mother had no idea I would not return with my aunt. It would be months before I would see my mother. My grandmother was pleased to have me with her, and we had a good life together. She read me stories about Jesus, made sure I said my prayers each night, and showered me with love. I had become hers.

My grandmother was known for her love of children and for taking in other people's children. Maybe it was because she had such difficulty having her own. She was married to her first husband at age 17 but didn't have any children until her thirties. In between, she suffered miscarriage after miscarriage and the deaths of two babies. The first children she raised were her first husband's three nieces. She loved them as if they had been carried in her womb. She later had eight children of her own, six who lived into adulthood. In addition to raising her two boys and four girls, she also raised three of her grandchildren.

In contrast to the Beaver's and Brady's, the daily life of my Georgia family operated quite differently. My grandmother rose daily before sunrise beginning her day with prayer, always giving thanks to God for life, reading her Bible, and preparing breakfast. She spent the rest of her day cleaning the house, feeding the chickens, sweeping the yard, and working in the field and then in her vegetable garden. After working outdoors, she would return to the house to finish preparing my granddaddy's dinner. She was creative and loved canning fruits and vegetables, creating wax flowers, sewing, and growing flowers. I was her helper and joined her to pick berries, to peel and prepare fruits and vegetables for canning, and to help her in the garden.

My grandfather worked on the land, planting, and plowing, and doing hard labor, cutting down oaks and pines off the family's property to be sold to the nearby lumberyards. My grandmother always had dinner waiting when my grandfather came home. He would have it no other way. Typical meals included cornbread, seasoned greens, beans, and any other vegetables that we raised on the farm. My grandfather preferred to eat meat at breakfast, and my grandmother often prepared stewed chicken, sausage, ham with red-eye gravy, grits, eggs, and biscuits. A hot breakfast awaited us every day.

As sweet as my grandmother was, my grandfather could be sour. He worked hard during the week and played hard on the weekend. During the week, he was very strict, and on the weekend, he found joy in a bottle. Obedience was crucial for him, and if you were disobedient, you wouldn't get a talking to, you would get a whipping. I didn't get them often, but when I did, I got them hard. Although he was strict, I loved my grandfather, who I saw as a giant. My favorite memory of my grandfather was our yearly trek to Greensboro, Georgia, to purchase my annual pair of Oxford saddle shoes. My grandfather insisted on the proper care of the shoes. I was never to slip my feet out without unlacing them and never, ever was I to walk on the heel of the shoe.

Granddaddy was tall, fit, with dark blue eyes, and strong. He was a man of many talents. He could build houses, slaughter animals, break in wild horses, dig graves, and plant and harvest crops, among other things. He was the person you called on to get whatever you needed to be done. He took care of his family and his community. He made me feel protected, if not loved, and that was important to me. As I grew older, however, I felt his rules too restrictive, I rebelled, and that created many tense moments in our relationship. But I was always proud to be his granddaughter. When meeting someone who asked who I was, I always replied - M. C. Turner's granddaughter.

My family in Washington, DC, lived a drastically different life from my Georgia family. There was no farm to tend, and the family consisted of a mother, father, and two children, plus me in the summers and a few holidays. I am not sure how the dynamics of the family shifted when I was there, but I am sure it changed. I was glad to be with my brother, who was two years younger than my sister, who was the youngest of the three. My sister had lived in Georgia with my grandparents and me from the age of three until she was seven when she decided she was slopping no more hogs and picking no more peas. When she left to return to DC, I was devastated. Although I didn't know why I realized that leaving grandma and granddaddy permanently was never an option I could consider. I was always glad to be with my siblings in the summers, but leaving my grandmother created turmoil in my heart. Each year when I left Georgia to be with my family in DC, I would cry all the way. Often flying in First Class to DC, I would sit sullenly with tears rolling down my cheeks, just thinking of my grandmother being all alone and how much I would miss her. I am sure my seatmate created stories of who I was and why I was crying. I always thought of grandmother being alone even though granddaddy was there. In my world, granddaddy didn't count as proper company for grandmother. This emotional crisis would be repeated upon my return to Georgia.

I also hated leaving my DC family. I would go through the same histrionics as when I left grandma. I always wanted everyone to be together. I felt my heart would break each leg of my journey. My Uncle Eddie, who lived in Cincinnati, upon reflecting on my pain, once said, "Why not let her be in one place so she wouldn't go through this trauma?" And trauma it was. However, after a few days, I would settle in. My mother and grandmother seemed radically different. I often wondered if they belonged to the same family. It wasn't easy to recognize that she was my grandmother's daughter. She looked more like her father's people. She was dark-skinned, robust, and tall. My grandmother was light-skinned and of medium build and short, maybe 5 feet tall, and she barely spoke above a whisper. My mother's voice was loud enough to raise the dead and became even louder when she was angry. She was very demanding and expected a lot from her children. In DC, I didn't have to work in a field, slop hogs, cut wood, and draw water from a well, but the beds had to be made, the bathroom cleaned, the house swept, garbage out, dog fed and food for dinner taken out of the freezer to thaw so she could cook when she came home. Before she arrived from work, we ran about making sure everything was done and up to her very high standard. We often wondered why we had to move the sofa to sweep under it every week. However, I loved having these chores divided by three. I now value my mother's sense of order that I rarely achieve. In the summer, I went from being an only child to the oldest sibling of three. However, I always thought of my brother, William, as the oldest. He was often my mother's enforcer and generally would give a full report on what the girls had not done when she came home.

The summers were active and fun. We often went on day trips. I remember going to Pennsylvania to visit Hershey Park and to Delaware to walk the boardwalk on Rehoboth Beach. There were also trips to Wild Wood and Atlantic City, New Jersey. During the week, we all headed to the bowling alley, and on the weekends, there was a softball game. The men played ball, and the women prepared hot dogs, hamburgers, and barbecue. I would attend concerts on the National Mall and in DuPont Park. I spent a lot of my time with an older cousin, who I thought of like a big sister. I inherited all of her hand me downs and proudly so. I often slept at her house and tagged along with her and her friends to the park, the neighborhood swimming pool, and parties. I felt privileged to have lived in two worlds. Most of all, I was glad to have the time to get to know my mother. I observed her often looking for me in her. Although she seemed hard as nails, I learned she was marshmallow inside.

She was outspoken and didn't seem to be afraid of anything. She was an activist at heart. She worked at United Airlines and often wielded a picket sign when as an employee, she and others felt they were not treated fairly. You could also find her in her kitchen styling some woman's hair or making barbecue and at church raising money for a project for the elderly that she had dreamed up. We had dinner each day sitting around the table. She wasn't a great cook like grandma, but she did ok to feed her family. This was my immediate impression after seeing her cook frozen collard greens from a box. That was nothing grandma ever did. My mother grew up as a tomboy, working with my grandfather plowing in the field and cutting down and trimming trees to take to the lumberyard. She wasn't domestic. She loved her extended family and was the glue that held them together. She stayed connected to her sisters and brothers and those aunts, cousins, and friends she had left behind in Georgia and those dispersed over the United States. She had everyone's telephone number memorized.

I never really questioned why my life was lived in two places. I wasn't the only one who shared the experience of living with grandparents while mothers were miles away. African American grandparents often lent a helping hand to their daughters, who had left the South for greater opportunities in the North. Many came to get their children when they were on their feet; others allowed their children to remain with their parents. It was often remarked by other older grandparents who were rearing their grandchildren, "As soon as the child can do something to help you, here come the mamas wanting them back." I was in love with my grandmother. I never wanted to leave her, and I think she never wanted me to go. My mother was very present in my life. She called often, spoiled me with beautiful clothes and lots of toys at Christmas. I lived with my grandparents until I graduated from high school and left to attend Clark College in Atlanta, Ga. That was where my destiny seemed good. I saw a bright future ahead, a degree, career, husband, house, and the family that I always desired where everyone was together.

My journey to the perfect family, I felt, was assured when I met a tall, handsome Morehouse College student who won my heart the first day we met. I met him waiting at a bus stop in downtown Atlanta. Neither of us had caught the bus before and were riding to a place we had never been. We talked for hours spending the day together. He was the perfect gentlemen, he treated me to lunch at Murray Subs, held my hand as we crossed the street, and listened to me as I talked on and on and on about everything under the sun. From that day forward, we were inseparable. He was smart, funny, adventurous, and a great listener. I was attracted to his kindness, and I knew one day we would be married. I readily thought of him as not only a good marriage partner but also great father material. I envisioned the three children we would have. I looked forward to realizing this dream. He had come from a large family. He had 5 siblings, and his mother, like my grandmother, cared for many children to whom she did not birth. His family gave me something I never had, a sense of what it was like to be a full member of a family and not just a visiting member. As a child living in two places, I always seemed a bit of an outsider.

When in Washington, DC, I was the country bumpkin, and when I was in Crawfordville, Georgia, I was teased as the city slicker. I was Carlos's wife, for better or worse. I loved it when his family came together. They shared amusing stories about their mom and dad and their childish escapades. Some of the stories seemed outlandish. My husband and his brothers spoke of climbing trees, sitting on a branch, cutting it down, and riding it down into the lagoon. Although he was from the Caribbean, and I was from the rural South, we had much in common. My imagination took flight, and I began to see our traditions and ways of being played out in the lives of our three children, the two girls, and one boy.

Carlos and I were married on June 25, 1984. We honeymooned in New Orleans because he wanted to go to the World's Fair. He loved science and acquiring knowledge. When we returned to Atlanta, we mapped out what was next for our lives, where we would live, what types of jobs we would pursue, and how we would include our families into our married lives. And we discussed having a baby. Although he said I was the only baby he needed, I ignored his sentiments and moved forward with my dreams and plans. I wanted to do everything right because this child would be the beginning of the family I dreamed of. I read all the pamphlets about pregnancy and childbirth. I made an appointment with a doctor to discuss pre-pregnancy planning. Everything appeared to be on track, I was healthy and seemed emotionally ready for the responsibility.

However, I began to have debilitating pains during my

menstrual cycle that took my attention away from getting pregnant. There were times when I would be on my knees because the pain was so intense. I went to doctor after doctor trying to find out what was wrong with me and what could stop the pain. I was given prescription-strength Tylenol and was told some women just have pain. Because I was also urinating 15 or more times a day, one doctor advised that my urethra was too small. To enlarge it, I had a procedure done every two weeks where my urethra was stretched with an iron rod. It was only when my insurance changed, and I had chosen another doctor that I was asked by the nurse practitioner, "Has anyone ever told you that you have fibroid tumors?" "No," I replied, somewhat alarmed. I had never heard of a fibroid tumor. She said one of the fibroids as large as a grapefruit and that it was sitting on my bladder, causing frequent urination.

Was it cancerous? Was I going to die? What did I need to do? Would I be able to have children? My mind went wild, thinking of a million questions. After nearly a year, I made the decision to have the tumors removed. The pain had become so intense that I would become temporarily blind, unable to see to drive home from work. The doctors assured me that the surgery to remove the fibroid tumors would not prevent me from having children. My mother said, leave them alone and that she had fibroids when she was pregnant with my sister. But the pain was unbearable. So, I went ahead with the surgery. Unfortunately, the surgery did not go as anticipated, and one of my fallopian tubes collapsed during the procedure. The doctor said it shouldn't prevent me from getting pregnant because I only needed one operative tube. However, we tried and tried, but no results. My husband was very supportive and tried to make me feel better by saying that just the two of us were family. He didn't know what a baby meant to me.

I had lived my life based on preparing for the children. Although I wanted to search for another job, I stayed where I worked because I thought it would be flexible enough for me to bring the baby to work. I purchased a Volvo sedan because I needed a safe car for the baby. I had a list of baby names. However, there was never a pregnancy,

SHAKING OFF THE DUST

and eight years later, after graduate school, promotions, and volunteer work, I was diagnosed with another fibroid. This one was bigger than the one they had removed years earlier. I quickly scheduled the surgery because the clock was ticking.

I was 27 when I started trying to have children, and now I was in my mid-thirties. This surgery was more tragic than the first. Yes, I had a fibroid tumor, but what was more heartbreaking was that I also had a cyst on my ovary that again was as big as a grapefruit that had to be removed. Removing this ovary, which was on the opposite side of the collapsed fallopian tube, took away any chance of me getting pregnant naturally. To cheer me up, I was told I had a beautiful uterus, and I was a great candidate for in-vitro fertilization. I sobbed as I listened to the doctor, tear apart my dreams and my future. There would be no baby. I would never have the family I desired. Carlos attempted to comfort me and shared with me the many rewards of not having children. His voice sounded like a nail on chalkboard. I wanted him to go away.

Over the years, I have been asked, inappropriately, why I didn't have children. I have been insulted because I didn't have children. I was thought to be a woman more interested in her career than in building a family. They didn't know my story but assumed my reality. I realized they were not being spiteful but were influenced by a patriarchal society that insists that a woman's worth is based on her youthfulness and her ability to produce children. In the Bible, and many cultures, having children was considered a blessing from God; barren women were looked down upon as being cursed and had little status in their communities. Friends advised me on rituals, prayers, and charms that could help me get pregnant. However, none of the rituals are good if you don't have the equipment.

Infertility in black women is not something that is often discussed. Those of us who are childless and wanted children are not very vocal. And our challenge is often overlooked. We are invisible. The attention is on the stereotype of being over sexual, highly fertile, and welfare

SHAKING OFF THE DUST

mothers.

Childless women often become the focus of attention when it surfaces that we don't have children. Mothers tell us to be glad and often, they offer us one of their children. And often, they offer us one of their children, "Come, they say you can have mine." This is followed by a litany of reasons why motherhood is so hard, and then they begin to display all the cute baby pictures. It's a mixed-up world. More African American women are sharing their stories and their heartbreaks about their inability to have children. It helps me to know that I wasn't alone in my feeling of being a woman but feeling not fully woman because I didn't have children. Listening to their stories echoes my pain and I feel less alone. I realized that the thoughts I had of not feeling fully woman because I didn't have children was engrained in my psyche. My dolls prepared me for motherhood. At a friend's hospital bed after her hysterectomy, all the pain of not having a child flooded back, and I was glad I could be there to comfort her. I could see the deep well of sadness in her eyes. It mirrored my own.

After the second surgery, I knew that for me to have a baby, it was going to take a miracle in the form of hard cash. I read about in-vitro fertilization, particularly the section that indicated that in-vitro was not covered by insurance. I would have to pay out of pocket. I also learned that most often, in-vitro did not work the first time and that it often took three attempts. And then I read that it cost thousands of dollars not secured by insurance. My husband and I were working every day, but we couldn't see where the money would come from, and once we paid for the in-vitro, what money would be left to actually raise the child. We decided that our lives could be full without a child

I had many reasons for wanting a biological child. I wanted someone who would carry on the story of my grandparents and be willing to cherish their legacy as much as I did. I wanted a child who could carry on the love my husband and I shared. I also wanted to leave something behind that indicated that I was here on this earth.

Carlos and I discussed adoption. He wasn't on board. If he was going to raise a child, he wanted it to be of his own blood. His mother agreed. I persisted. Friends had recently adopted from a non-traditional agency, and I thought that would be a good fit for us. It took a while to convince Carlos. In fact, he brought me a puppy to help take my mind off adoption. He thought that the puppy would provide a distraction. I loved the puppy, but that made me want a child even more. I could see him or her playing with our dog. I finally persuaded Carlos to adopt. We completed the application and made an appointment to speak with the attorney.

Although things didn't work out as I had planned, I was grateful for the opportunity to be an adoptive mother. I began to think that I was adopted by my grandparents and realized how grateful I was for the sacrifice they made to raise me. And before the adoption was final, my world fell apart when my husband's kidneys failed, and he was immediately placed on dialysis.

Everything changed in an instant. I couldn't think about adopting a baby because my big baby needed me. As if someone heard me and decided to rearrange my plans, the lawyer called and informed us that they were no longer handling adoptions. Between my husband's health and my shattered dreams, I wasn't sure what to do and where to stand, and what would happen to me. But I did know that I was with my family and that it didn't take an infant to fulfill my dream. My husband and I and the dog Mango made up Carlos and Angela Rice's immediate family. My thought was, as long as the two of them were in my life, I would be ok. I wasn't prepared for either one of them leaving.

Mango, my sweet companion of 16 years, started having severe health problems, and I had to put him down in 2010. I heaved with tears as I soothed him as the veterinarian gave him a lethal dose to help him rest forever. I was grateful for all the joy he had given me. He was more than a pet. He was my dog child. From him, I learned a lot about the transcendent power of love. Now, it was just Carlos and me to look forward to our golden years. I dreamed of us traveling to the countries we had yet to visit, moving to the rural community where I had grown up, and spending time together growing vegetables and raising goats or pigs. The thought of us spending our days and nights together made me feel giddy with anticipation.

I could see my husband with his cap cocked on the side of his head, just as my grandfather used to wear his. He was retired, and I looked forward to early retirement as well. But that dream was canceled when my heart was torn apart when my husband Carlos was diagnosed with brain cancer, glioblastoma multiforme, stage four. Over our thirty plus years together, we had gone through a series of health challenges, and through the grace of God, we had come through on the other side. Although the doctor predicted that Carlos had only a year to live, we didn't give up. We prayed. I prayed and invited people from all across the globe to pray for him and read scripture to him each day. I played healing music, accepted the help of a friend who placed him on a raw food diet, anointed his head and rubbed his feet each day with frankincense oil, took him to an herbalist twice or more a week. But all failed, and I, with no other choice, had to say so long to the love of my life, my teacher, and my friend. All ideas of creating the perfect family dissolved in front of my eyes. All of my plans for the future went up in smoke. I was alone. Carlos was great at reassuring me that all was well just the two of us. But he never prepared me for him not being here. As I go about my day to day dealing with being alone, being a widow, the reality of not having children sets in. There is no one who stops in to check on "mom" or any grandchildren to brag about. As I chat with my friends, they share pictures of their grandchildren, prepare for their daughter's weddings, and family vacations. I stand aside, recognizing that once again, I'm the outsider, the free one, responsible only for myself. But I realize that I am equipped, I. am the one my grandmother called peculiar. Perhaps growing up as an only child, when I had a brother and sister; growing up with grandparents when I had parents; living between urban and rural; and being both

SHAKING OFF THE DUST

familiar and stranger made me a little peculiar.

I realized that maybe, in some way, I had sent forth mixed messages to the Universe. As a young woman, as much as I enjoyed the thought of one day becoming a mother, the idea of getting pregnant was one of the worst things that could happen to me – it meant death. I saw girls give up their dreams because of an unexpected pregnancy. Perhaps I sent the message, no baby here. The idea of getting pregnant before marriage was one of the worst things that could happen to me. I sent the message "no baby here."

I recognized as my spiritual teaching expresses that our thoughts have power. And perhaps when I was a child, my love of babies was related to the idea of one day having something that I believed truly belonged to me.

Today, looking back, I have released the dust of creating the perfect family and the sense of not belonging. I have decided that I am whole, fully woman, complete just as I am. I am grateful for the many families that have influenced who I am today, the Turner family, the

Harrington family, the Rice family, and many other families that I have accepted into my life and in some ways co-created and nurtured. I belong to them. They are all part of who I am.

There are two definitions of family. A group consisting of a parent and children living in one household. The second definition is all the descendants of a common ancestor. There is a third definition that is not there, all that is infused with Spirit. Therefore, family all are we.

No, Jackrabbits don't drive cars. I never birthed a child. But I have birthed creative ideas and dreams that have nourished my soul, and I hope, inspired, and encouraged others.

7

SHADOW LIFE

When I was nine years old, I said to my mother, "I wish you never had me." I think I just wanted to hurt my mother at that moment. When I was a teen, I often thought of death and dying. My pain was real, but it was not severe enough to make me want to leave the earth. So, I stayed. I could never bring such pain to my parents. As I got older, there were times that such thoughts resurfaced. How could I leave my children?

At six-thirty that Monday evening, he pulls up to the bus stop and offers me a ride home from the temporary job I had taken to help a neighbor. I accept. He looks like someone I know from the neighborhood, so I get into the front seat when he leans over and opens the passenger door. Immediately, he turns the car around and heads away from the city. "You're going in the wrong direction," I say.

He does not look at me; he keeps driving to a destination only he knows. The heavily traveled road seems suddenly still and eerily quiet. I feel alone. My vision blurs. Am I crying? I don't hear myself. Thoughts are rushing through my jumbled mind as quickly as he is speeding to his appointed place. What is this man going to do to me? Will he kill me like that man killed my classmate? I don't want to die. Where am I? Do I fight? How will I get home? How will my parents react if I tell, and what will they think of me? I look back to the city as it fades into a disappearing horizon. I am adrift inside a maze of feelings as I stare ahead on a ride that leads to a life of secret sorrow.

He turns off the main highway onto a dirt road and drives less than a mile into a wooded area where he stops the car. There are no houses. He turns and slides towards me. I start screaming and yelling, "Don't do this to me. Please take me back to the bus stop. You wouldn't want this to happen to your sister." I keep talking in the hopes that the young black man would have pity on me and let me go. I had hoped that he had a sister, mother, or someone he loved. How could he do this to me, a young girl he did not know? How could he do this to anyone?

When my words go unheard, I start screaming, flailing my arms, trying to hit his face. "Shut up and stop fighting," he orders as he grabs my arms and pins them with his weight. He then reaches under the car seat and pulls out a pistol. He shows me the gun but does not point it at me; however, I am frightened more than I have ever been before. I think he is going to kill me.

I remain fully clothed. He pulls my underwear to the side and tries desperately to penetrate me. With my might, I stiffen my body, hold my breath, and push against him as he bangs against me with the stiff penis until he gives up.

Suddenly, saying nothing, he gets up and turns the sedan back toward the highway. "Where are you taking me?" I whimper.

"I'm taking you home," he says as he stares straight ahead. What does he mean? My home or his? "Where do you live?" he asks. I do not want him to know where I live, so

I don't give him the name of my street. I need to get close enough to home where I can walk. I glance down at the white button-down shirt now pulled from my skirt. My white blazer has smudges from the scuffle. I cannot get on the bus looking like this. I give him the name of a street that is close enough to where I live so that I can walk. I need to think. Since it is dark now, no one will notice me. He drives to the corner where I direct him and lets me out of the car, asking to see me again as though we are on a date. I mumble something and wait for him to drive off. My head is spinning, and my body aches. I stand on the sidewalk in a haze, not sure of which way to turn. After I steady myself, I walk home. I tell no one.

Days later, I say to an older friend, "I had a horrible dream." At first, I wonder if I dreamed of the assault. I want to think that it was a dream. After I finish summarizing what happened, leaving out some of the details, Sandra lowers her head, raises her eyes, and looks at me with skepticism. She says, "You better tell your mother."

Does she think that I would ever do that? What could my mother do? What could anyone? I cannot. My mother would scold me for accepting a ride with a stranger. She may feel for me and be angry at the attacker, but I know that she would blame me. She had taught me better. My daddy would want to find the attacker and kill him. He still saw me as his little girl, and I did not want him to see me in any other way. That night, I decided that I would never tell anyone ever again. After all, I had accepted the ride.

It is Tuesday, the day after the assault, and I feel different, but not in a way that I can define. I am still in shock and disbelief. Even though I do not want to, I go back to that job to let Mrs. Smith know that I cannot work for her any longer. I owe her that. Besides, I cannot let my neighbor, Joyce, down. She needed me to hold the position for her. I cannot cause her to lose the job. Mrs. Smith tells me that it is okay if I can't finish out the week.

She had always taken me to the bus stop, but on this day, she turns to her husband, who has come home from work early, and says, "Honey, drive her to the bus stop while I finish dinner." I don't know him. I do not want to get in the car with him or with any man; however, he honors his wife's request without hesitation. My fear intensifies as I open the Volkswagen door and get into the back seat. He drives along the route to the bus stop, but since it is late, he decides to drive me home. "I don't mind waiting for the bus," I say. He drives a few blocks and turns onto a side street where he stops.

Time stops; I cannot breathe. Mr. Smith whirls around and looks at me. It is dark now. Does he see the fear in my eyes? Does he care? He places his hand on my knee slightly underneath my skirt. I can't believe it is happening again. I hear the thump, thump, thump of my heart, and feel its vibrations in my throat and my ears. I am paralyzed. The hand stays on my right knee while its owner considers for a moment. Maybe he is pondering the ramifications of what might happen. I do not know. He ultimately turns around and drives. I exhale and give thanks.

For the next month leading up to graduation, I live and

function in a weird place, one where I have never been before. What little joy and happiness I had as I anticipated senior activities and graduation have evaporated like a fine mist. I go to the prom because my mother paid the dressmaker to work her magic on the white gown I had designed. It had an organza over-skirt trimmed in gold. My aunt had bought my shoes and accessories. If I did not go, they would be more than disappointed with me. I do not accept an invitation from the boy I dated earlier in the year. Instead, I go with friends. Somehow, I focus on schoolwork, pass my examinations, and graduate with my parents sitting together, even though they separated when I was three.

I love living in Memphis, where I attend school during the week. But now I am anxious to leave this city and go to my mother's house in the country for a summer of gardening, housework, and cooking. I am not excited about the work. Yet, I leave the city and go off to my country-life, which only lasts a few days. Then I am whisked back to the city where I live-in and take care of a two-year-old girl. My mother wants me to have a summer job that pays. Since my job opportunities in the country are limited, I go without protest. I do not want to live with anyone other than my family, but I need the money to buy clothing and supplies for college.

While living with the young white woman, her child, and her lover, I experience two other moments where I felt threatened with potential sexual assault. I feel uncomfortable when I learn that a man also lives in the small two-bedroom apartment. My mother did not know that when she secured the job for me, and I never told her. His demeanor quickly allays my fears. He pays me no attention. It is two other men who work for him that exhibit inappropriate behavior toward me on different occasions when I am alone. Even though neither goes beyond words and lecherous looks to actions, I feel scared, ashamed, and helpless. My feelings are the same during the assault and each threatening encounter that I experienced.

I did not have the language or the thought process to inform me as to what had happened that left me exposed, vulnerable, and thoroughly afraid. After other uncomfortable situations with men throughout the years, I started to believe that such behaviors were commonplace, and that girls and women just had to endure them. Furthermore, what rights did a black girl living in the South have when Jim Crow was strutting around, devising ways to keep black people from advancing? Anyway, who would listen to a black girl accusing white men of such behavior?

I stay busy doing nothing but work, no time for friends and fun. No alone time. I push my feelings down so completely that I think I am alright and in no need of healing. Where can I go? Who can I tell? I believe that I am living the way I should, yet I have no joy, no real interest in anything. I go off to college somewhat unwillingly as my heart and mind are not in it. I am living for my parents. Both are educators who have plans for me that don't coincide with mine. I withhold much of myself and my dreams, which may have conditioned me for a lifetime of keeping secrets. In college, I go through the motions attending classes and making friends, but I am empty inside, even depressed. Periodically, I threated to drop out.

Just three years after entering college, I am newly married and moving more than 600 miles away from my family. I know no one in my new hometown except my husband. Moving into the small apartment is not difficult since we do not have many belongings; nevertheless, after a busy day of putting things in order, I feel exhausted. I go to bed at ten and immediately fall asleep. Although I am sleeping, I have an inner feeling to raise my head from the pillow and look around. I think I see something in the bathroom, which is across the hall. The bathroom light is on. What I think I see looks like a plaid cloth slightly protruding from behind the half-opened door. It all seems strange, like a dream. I do not recall putting anything on that door. I blink and fall back onto the pillow, overcome by my need for sleep.

Suddenly, I am wide awake. When I recognize that someone is in my room, I scream, but no one can hear me. I realize that no one is going to hear me because I live at the end of the row of five single-story townhomes. The house next door is vacant, and Maria, across the walk, has gone to Puerto Rico to visit her family while her husband is at sea. Still, I scream as loud as I can. I call out "JESUS!" When the assailant falls on top of me, I see the glimmer of steel in the moonlight filtering through the window. I feel the cold metal press against my neck. "Stop screaming," he demands, "or I will cut your throat."

"Don't hurt me," I plead "I'm pregnant." Not knowing the time, I say, "My husband is on his way home." That does not seem to matter to him. He rips my pink pajama pant off and attempts to penetrate me. I keep pleading with him to leave, "My husband will soon be home from work." The flaccid penis does not respond to his violent behavior. He pushes my head towards his groin. I resist and try to reason with him. "I know you don't want to do this," I cry. I do not know the time, but I know it is late, so I keep pleading and stalling. Again, I say, "My husband will be home soon." The assailant probably knows what time it is and the time my husband gets home. He gives up.

Shortly after he leaves through the back door, I hear my husband enter through the front. I have stripped the sheets from the bed and am in the bathroom, desperately trying to wash away the crime from my body. I do not want to, but I have to tell him what happened. Neither of us knows what to do. I want to settle down and sleep. My devoted and frightened husband feels awful about not being there to protect me. He must to do something to fix me, to make my pain go away. He drives me to the Air Force infirmary to get a sedative. I cannot talk, think, or feel. I need the night to end.

And so, on that hot night in June, I take the pill and sleep.

A few nights after the attack around ten o'clock, someone knocks at the back door. I cannot imagine who it is, but I am not going to open the door. I yell, "Who is it?" The voice on the other side sends shivers through me. It is the attacker's voice. I will never forget it. I make sure the door is locked; I place a kitchen chair under the doorknob, and I go into the bedroom and lock the door. How must it have been for my foremothers to be awakened in the night by a rapist? Did they cry out to their fathers, brothers, husbands? Did they call out to Jesus?

I hear that voice again as I walk past its house. It belongs to a young white man who must have channeled his forefathers' wicked designs for African treasure. I pass the house as though it is a confederate monument, without looking.

On a cold night in December, I deliver a stillborn baby.

Again, I bury my feelings for the sake of designing a lifestyle. I live as though I am okay. Neither my husband nor I ever bring up the assault after that night. It is as though that horrible night disappeared from our collective memory.

We don't tell our children how we lost the sister they never got to meet.

That assault is devastating to my whole being. I am a wreck. The infant growing inside of me never moves as a healthy baby does. I learned that later after I became pregnant with my other children.

Whenever I saw a door slightly open, it would transport me back to that horrible night. Most nights, I feel compelled to stay awake and wait for my husband to come home. Otherwise, I sleep with the bedroom door locked.

Did the medicine that I took to calm my nerves and help me sleep cause my baby to be stillborn? I do not know, but I have always wondered.

Perhaps my daughter decided that this world is too cruel for her.

For years, I am not sure of my worth. Those assaults change the trajectory of my life. Who am I supposed to be? I was on track to become a teacher like my parents. I often played school when I was a child, and I was always the teacher. As I get older, I don't embrace that career path, but I teach for a while until I discover something more exciting and suitable for my temperament. I struggle internally with the feelings which set me on my new life's path. My secrets push me into the shadows and completely redefine me and my goals. I am no longer interested in pursuing a career other than that of wife and mother. I find joy and satisfaction in those two roles. The world outside has no appeal for me. I try outwardly to live as though nothing has happened. My method of coping with the trauma is to suppress it and keep busy with activity.

Sometimes I convince myself that the first assault did not occur. I cannot deny the second.

Life presented me with situations that were, at first, perplexing, and then unfair. At least, that was how I felt then, so I looked for answers through Bible study and religion as a young wife and mother. I learned that life is full of experiences that can bring challenges that are sometimes difficult to understand and even more difficult to face and overcome. Each negative experience was equal to collecting dust on my spirit. That dust built up over the years and hindered my progress. I needed to remove it and move on with life in the best way possible. I had faith that there were solutions to my problems. Sometimes there were setbacks and times when I had to shake it off and move on.

Jesus told his disciples when he sent them out to preach his kingdom message that if a house or city did not welcome them to "shake off the dust from their fee" as they leave. In effect, to let all harmful traces of the encounter go and move on to another town and another home. Shaking off the dust of assault and the resulting trauma can be challenging. I had to acknowledge and confront the possibility that something psychologically damaging happened to me during my childhood before the first assault I can't identify what occurred that caused me to block out a year of my life other than sexual abuse. Perhaps it conditioned me to be further traumatized through sexual assault.

I was functioning the best I knew how with anger simmering beneath the surface. Those events changed me. I did not live up to my potential or my mother's expectations. I coped by doing what I term busy-work, which entailed household chores and home improvements, taking classes. I longed for perfection in some areas of my life, even though I knew that it was unknowable and unattainable. I thought I could be the perfect wife and mother. Of course, that was not possible. If I was not involved in some productive activity, I felt useless. I did not know how to relax and enjoy life until most of it was spent.

As time passed, I started reading and searching for answers. In the late 1980s, more than twenty years after the first assault, I decided to acknowledge what had happened to me; I came out as a victim so that I could regain my power. I responded to a newspaper advertisement for Rape Crisis Counselors thinking that in helping others, I could help myself. The training was educational and therapeutic. I learned that sex crimes, including rape and sexual abuse, were prevalent throughout the community affecting all ages, races, and socioeconomic groups. I was not alone. I interviewed and trained without disclosing any details other than that I had been a victim for too many years. It was then that I became a survivor. My victimization had allowed me to become an empathic listener, a necessary skill when working with victims. I learned not to judge other women and what they did to survive.

Many rape cases happened during youth, yet women in their thirties and beyond were still suffering the psychological aftermath. Unless the pain is deeply embedded and hidden in the subconscious mind, it nags at the survivor. The trauma of the assault can surface when there is a cue in her environment, such as a smell, sound, movie, joke, or anniversary date that takes a survivor back to the distressing experience.

In the late 1980s and early 1990s, statistics reported that rape affected one in four women. Since most crimes go unreported, many victims find ways to function in families, jobs, and other areas of life. They may not reach their full potential, but they do more than survive. If every woman who experienced sexual abuse or assault of any kind remained a victim unable to work, manage a family, and function socially because she could not cope, society would fall apart. On the flip side, if prisons could contain every man who committed some form of sexual misbehavior, abuse, or assault, society would collapse.

Sexual misconduct and sex crimes are pervasive in government, education, the military, medicine, religion, industry, sports, entertainment, and on and on. Many organizations are complicit in harboring and protecting perpetrators of sex crimes.

There needs to be punishment for rape and sexual abuse. Men who stop short of rape must also answer for their actions. The punishment must fit the crime. On average, there are 321,500 victims, 12 years or older, of rape and sexual assault each year in the United States, according to Rape, Abuse & Incest National Network (RAINN).

While sexual assault and or abuse may not destroy the body, they can damage, delay, or impair potential. They can cause a complete redefinition of self and goals. Assault can damage and even destroy self esteem. Sex crimes can altogether disable any woman if she does not find ways to cope.

After suffering assault, women have cleaned themselves up and moved on with their lives for centuries. What were their other options?

Keeping secrets damages the soul and can change the course of one's life. I believe that I was held captive by my secrets and lived a shadow-life for many years. Secrets changed who I was and influenced who I was to become. Living a shadow-life affected how I saw myself and my interactions and relationships with others. I have struggled and tried to overcome the traumatic events of my past— the pain, shame, and embarrassment of sexual assault. I felt the guilt associated with rape throughout most of my life. Why did I get into that car? I knew better. Why didn't I wait for the bus? Why didn't I listen to my inner voice in both instances? I should have made sure the windows were closed and locked. What I have found is that the past demands a constant reckoning. Whatever I have experienced in life is still with me, not as a constant companion, but in a way that requires more of my attention than I should have to devote to it.

Sexual assault, at any age, is the most intimate way to affect a person with long-lasting pain. The effects of sexual abuse, sexual assault, and rape cut deep into the core of who we are as individuals. It is different from physical assault in that it carries a stigma. It involves degradation, shame, and often blame. Society has placed nearly as much blame on the victim as on the perpetrator in many cases. People often judge a woman's attire, behavior, or an unwise decision she makes, such as accompanying a young man to his apartment, accepting a drink, a date, or a ride home. Those judgments again victimize her. Her unwise decision should not cause her to lose her peace of mind and sense of safety, her self esteem, her virginity, or her life. Some people believe that women "invite" rape by dressing sexy or "provocative" by flirtatious behavior or by going out alone at night. Others think a victim's physical attractiveness, such as her voluptuous body, causes a man to rape her. Neither of those attributes matter. She also does not have to fit a "type." She is still vulnerable to rape. Rape victims are as young as a few months and as old as their eighties. Mentally challenged women, disabled women, women in nursing homes, and homeless women are also victimized. Men are responsible for their own behavior.

America—its justice system and its men— enabled sexual crimes for centuries. Law enforcement has not adequately dealt with women's accusations. In early America, the master had his way with an enslaved woman. After all, she was his property. He had bought her. The white woman was also treated as property and relegated to a similar position when it came to saying "no" to the white man. Little has changed.

Sexual flirtation is often tolerated and even accepted as part of a man's nature. Perhaps it is looked upon as a rite of passage. Some of the sexually tinged behaviors—a pat on the butt and an unwanted hug or kiss —are even expected and sanctioned by statements such as "boys will be boys," "locker-room talk," and "boy talk."

Now we are in the Me Too and Times Up movements. Me Too, founded by Tarana Burke and magnified by famous Hollywood stars, deals with sexual violence against women. It put the world on notice that sexual violence needs to end. Times Up focuses on a safe workplace free from gender-based discrimination and sexual harassment and assault. These two movements empower victimized women and serve to educate the community. They have encouraged a national reckoning with a dirty "big" secret held by too many Americans.

There have been many perpetrators and even more victims for too many years. Many of those who are not victims, perpetrators, or someone who knew or worked with either, were probably shocked by the recent revelations made by women against wealthy and powerful men.

I am perplexed as to why men feel a need to control women. But since we live in a male-dominated society, it seems that men do think that it is a "man's world." Being such, they employ their physical strength, social status, professional position, and charm to take sexual advantage of trusting women. Usually, such men are weak, afraid, often impotent, and sometimes themselves victims. Young boys and men are also victims of sexual abuse and rape.

Men who rape need to feel powerful. Some are responding to anger and disappointment in their personal lives, where they have little or no control. They prey on women they can dominate, if only for a short time. Whatever the reason a man sexually assaults a woman, the aftermath is something that the woman may deal with for many years. Some assaults are so violent that victims may never fully recover.

When we let go of the idea that "rape is sex," then it will be easier to prosecute such crimes in the court of law and the court of opinion. It will remove the stigma so the victim can report the act as an assault wherein the perpetrator used his penis as a weapon. The penis, when used to attack, is indisputably a weapon just as a hand, a gun, a knife, or any other instrument used to commit violence against another individual. Sexual assault may or may not include physical force. It can be the result of coercion, pressure, and intimidation as with a family member, employer/employee, or any interaction where there is familiarity and an unequal power dynamic.

I suggest that we focus more attention on the word —

assault⎮ when working with a victim. The term "sex" sends

the mind in a direction that lessens the impact of the crime.

All crime is detrimental to women; however, excluding

murder, sex crimes are the most destructive. Rape and

sex crimes are harmful on a psychological and physical

level. Victims of assault can experience Post Traumatic

Stress Disorder (PTSD) similar to that experienced by

combat veterans. If not dealt with effectively, such trauma

can manifest in many negative behaviors such as drug

and alcohol abuse, overeating, and promiscuity. PTSD

can cause anxiety, flashbacks, depression, and suicidal

ideation.

Although neither assailant penetrated my body and

completed the sex act, I felt as though each had raped me.

I saw myself as a rape victim for most of my life. Initially,

I suffered intense guilt over accepting the ride. Despite

my mother's admonition and my inner warning, I took the

ride. I also did not check the window to see if it was locked

before I went to bed. That guilt became anger, not against

the attackers, but me. I experienced anxiety and depression characteristic of rape victims.

When I look back to when I was seventeen, I do not feel sorry for the woman I am today. I feel a deep sadness and sorrow for that 17-year-old girl who anticipated stepping into the world on her terms. She was an idealist who imagined her perfect world where men knew how to treat women. Her father, grandfathers, and uncles, presented positive images of men. She went on to meet other young men who were respectful, moral, and decent, including the man she married.

The later assault destroyed my unborn daughter and cheated my family and me out of knowing her. It upended my view of men, making me suspicious of them and even fearful of some. For a while, I wondered if most men were waiting, like wild animals stalking prey, for an opportunity to assault women.

Today, there are many community resources to deal with emotional concerns. Emotional issues were not discussed or addressed in any way during my youth. I knew nothing about the mental health system. People handled their mental and emotional issues in personal ways. It never occurred to me that I should seek counseling. I knew that I needed to fix myself. The only way I knew to do that was through religion. I grasped the first religion that came along; however, it was overly restrictive and did not encourage thinking critically, confronting situations and challenges, and working through them. It was ineffective in clearing my mind and spirit of the effects of those damaging experiences, and it did not offer perspective or give me direction in my life. I believed that for me to clear up issues in my life, I needed to go to the root and understand why I experienced such. What could I learn from them , and how could I integrate them into my life? I needed to control my life without allowing adverse circumstances to derail me from my intentions. In exploring religion and spirituality, I took lessons from different paths to support my growth.

I later learned that our DNA contains unresolved issues

passed on by our ancestors, which can become ours. As such, it is incumbent on each of us to confront those issues that arise, so we do not continue to pass them on. In other words, we must break the cycles, which include generational rape and abuse. We must shake it off so that it will not affect another generation. I, a woman of African ancestry, have much trauma from my ancestors' captivity and the enslavement they experience in America to remove from my DNA.

In my youth, I thought I was shaking off the dust when I suppressed the memories of my attack. For a time, I thought I had overcome. I designed a lifestyle by consciously and consistently pushing down the feelings that could have paralyzed me. I felt an inner motivation to keep moving forward. I had observed my mother cope with physical, emotional, and financial adversity for years. She never stopped to wallow in her pain or to give it much attention. She often said that she could not afford to be sick. Mom had to shake it off and go to work regardless of how she felt. I do not know if her behavior unconsciously conditioned me or if I just wanted to imitate her. Perhaps I wanted to be reliable and as invincible as I thought she was.

My mother's and other black women's idea of therapy was to visit a sister or a girlfriend and talk for hours until they turned their problems, failures, fears, disappointments, and sorrows into tears and laughter. That Depression Era generation of black women seemed to endure burdens that I did not want to tolerate for a lifetime.

I feel that I am only now shaking off the dust of my secret past, which has held me captive for too long as I write the words on these few pages. I need to put my story outside of myself. As portrayed in the Bible, I am "shaking off the dust" of secrecy, shame, guilt, sadness, disappointment, and embarrassment. I am moving out of the shadows and into the light. It is happening for me, and I pray that it can happen for others.

8

In The Time of COVID-19

Sistah Scribes met in person in February for the last time before COVID-19 (Coronavirus Disease, 2019) interrupted their lives and caused them to shelter in their homes. Fear of getting the virus and spreading it required all people to wear masks, keep at least six feet apart, and to practice good handwashing habits. Nearly everything, except grocery and drug stores, shut down, including doctors' offices, out of fear of spreading the virus.

This worldwide pandemic got our attention like nothing else. The world went on hiatus – malls, concerts, sporting events, theatres, airports, restaurants, and entertainment venues shut their doors one day at closing time and did not open them for weeks and even months—those who could work from home did. Schools and colleges closed, and many teachers took their classrooms online. Some churches held virtual services, including weddings and funerals.

When our champions of Civil Rights – Rev. Joseph Lowery, Rev. C. T. Vivian, and Congressman John Lewis died, people tuned in to virtual services on-line and on television to celebrate their lives and to give them the honor and respect that they deserved.

Sistah Scribes continued their work on Shaking Off the Dust: Personal Narratives of Triumph using text messages, email, and Zoom. They seriously missed the camaraderie that meeting in person gave them, however, seeing one another on Zoom helped a bit.

The time has been challenging for many people, like parents who became school teachers overnight, in some cases teaching more than one child and one grade, restless teens who miss their friends, and working mothers who need daycare for young children. Then some that could not work from home or would not get a paycheck. Many food banks opened with lines stretching miles.

The time of COVID-19 has caused much hardship.
Yet, it has inspired much good and creativity in people
throughout the world. Neighbors have gotten to know one
another from a distance; professional musicians, actors,
and others have entertained from their balconies and living
rooms without charging. Many people have made masks
to sell or give away. Some made masks to give to the
homeless. The good that has come out of this pandemic is
too great to itemize. The environment became cleaner as
pollution decreased with limited human activity. Animals,
vegetation, and humans could breathe a little easier for a
while.

Sadly, some small business went under due to limited
operating capital. Some new on-line companies sprang
up to meet the needs of this time. People discovered new
interests, such as baking, gardening, and various hobbies.
The home-building stores remained open to provide
supplies for building, painting, and planting. It was a time
to catch up on home projects that had long been ignored.
For some, this has been a time of turning attention to

our health. We continued or started working out at home or walking in our communities. It has been a time for contemplating and meditating on what is essential in our lives. Some took stock of their lives and set new goals. Others planned what they will do when the pandemic ends. Many look forward to seeing extended family, traveling, attending weddings, and other celebrations in person. Proms, graduation ceremonies, holidays, and rituals that bring us together have been greatly missed. Virtual attendance is good, but not enough to satisfy the spirit.

The pandemic has also focused attention on many problems that plague our nation and the world. Healthcare is a more significant issue now as many people who are sick from COVID-19 are black and brown citizens who cannot afford insurance. They are dying from the virus in large numbers. Government funds have not prevented many people from sinking deeper into poverty.

The unjust treatment of African Americans by police and white vigilantes continued with the murders of George Floyd and Breonna Taylor. It brought to light the killing of

Armaud Arbery by vigilantes and Elijah McClain, a young violinist unjustly killed by police. Those murders woke the consciousness of humanity. People throughout the world of all races, ages, backgrounds chanted, "Black Lives Matter" (BLM). Those who did not understand systemic racism before COVID-19 now have some knowledge of what African Americans have experienced for generations. Symbols of white supremacy, in the form of statues and monuments, came falling down like Humpty Dumpty, but more needs to happen to make the system fairer for all.

People paid attention as various signs of blatant racism reared its ugly head. For example, when Bubba Wallace, an African American NASCAR driver, found a noose in his garage. What a beautiful sight it was to see the drivers in their colorful uniforms following Richard Petty, one of the greats of NASCAR, as they escorted and supported Bubba and pushed his car to the starting grid at Talladega.

COVID-19 is a wake-up call that some will heed, but others may decide to return to life as it was before the pandemic, if that is possible.

Our thoughts are with all who have suffered the effects of COVID-19, especially to those who have lost loved ones. We continue to pray for health and wholeness for our country and the world. We thank doctors, nurses, and all hospital staff, first responders, and every "essential" worker.

AFTERWORDS

Shaking Off the Dust: Personal Narratives of Triumph is a victory for each of the women who make up Sistah Scribes, the women's writing circle that came together to write and publish this volume of real-life stories. Their desire to share their personal experiences and to write other stories would not desist but sounded louder and louder, beckoning them to stop procrastinating, to liberate themselves from the tyranny of self-doubt and the idea that they were just too busy.

Time was also a charmer that lured them out of complacency by showing them the perils of not taking steps toward realizing the stirrings of their collective soul. They heard within themselves, "If not now, when." Sistah Scribes began to see clearly that the time is now.

As a way to encourage writing and publishing our individual projects, Shaking Off the Dust: Personal Narratives of Triumph was born to give each woman a safe space to explore her feelings and an opportunity to write and publish the experience as a group. It seemed a daunting task and a risky pursuit, but we gained significant insights and lessons that will help as we continue to write and publish our individual works.

Work on this project gave our monthly gatherings greater focus. We had our eyes set on an achievable goal, and it brought us together with a mission. This took place against the backdrop of delicious food, thought-provoking conversation, and exciting and relaxing retreats in beautiful locations. We developed trust and strengthened our friendship while having fun. Our greatest gift was getting our project done.

We hope Shaking Off The Dust: Personal Narratives of Triumph will encourage you to write, share, or start your group. You can connect with us by visiting www.sistahscribes.net or by emailing us at www.sistahscribes@gmail.com. Let this compilation be a catalyst to help you step out and follow the call of your soul.

Angella Vincentie Bramwell, LCSW was born in Jamaica. She has been a Licensed Clinical Social Worlker for over 28 years providing therapeutic support for individuals and families in crisis. Some of her other interests include traveling, metalsmithing, gardening, folk art and sewing. She lives in Atlanta, Georgia.

Angela Harrington Rice is a minister at heart. She is the Founder of One Love Spiritual Center and the creator of Widow Wings, a resiliency group for widows. Angela, formerly hosted A Woman's Place, an award-winning television talk show, which featured guests such as Susan Taylor, Iyanla Vanzant, Marianne Williamson, and other notables. Her first book, *Resurrecting the Lives of Liberated Women*, pays homage to women who inspired her. She has a BS, Mass Communications, MA, African American Studies and is studying for an MDiv degree.

Rev. Marcia White Laster is a minister, educator, spiritual counselor, and writer. She is a master teacher whose passion is for everyone to realize their highest potential. A passionate educator for over 45 years, she held management positions in museum education, higher education, and business in NYC, Tampa, and Atlanta. BA (Honors) Education, Ordained Minister, Spiritual Counselor/Life Coach, Barbara King School of Ministry, Atlanta, GA. She enjoys running, gardening, reading and traveling.

Barbara Gray Armstrong is the author of H*onoring My Journey: Memoir/Family History: An Angel Lit Our Way!* published in *Woman's World Magazine, 07/17/2017: Blog*, **www. honoringmyjourney.com**. She is a former educator, victim counselor/advocate, community volunteer, and activist who loves being wife/mother/grandmother, gardener, and world traveler. Barbara lives in Stone Mountain, GA., with her husband. She has a BA, English, and MS, Counseling.

Patricia Desamours has had a love affair with writing since third grade when she wrote a "book" entitled All About Me to fulfill a class assignment. Many decades later, Patricia is still writing every day as a working journalist. But, now she primarily tells other people's stories. Patricia lives and works in Atlanta. She enjoys traveling to warm, sunny climates, scuba diving, and baking.

DeAnna Park-Jones is a Realtor, Naturopathic Practitioner, Workshop Facilitator, and Writer. Through workshops, she empowers participants to tap into their creative purposes and manifest more abundance in their lives. As a Realtor, she connects homeownership as a pathway to holistic well-being and financial empowerment. DeAnna loves life! You might find her running a 26-mile marathon in Hawaii, doing comedy on the Atlanta Punchline stage, or spending time with her talented family and gifted Grands!

**Sheryl M. Johnson**, BS Psychology, MA counseling, certified spiritual counselor, ordained minister, healer, teacher, people person. A southern girl raised in NY suburbs. She is a world traveler and is always looking to see the good in every situation. Spirit-led and Spirit-driven. Life without end, Amen.

Made in the USA
Monee, IL
04 November 2020